THE POWER WITHIN

365 Day Devotional For Women

With *Love* All Things Are Possible

BY
SUSAN WRIGHT

Table of Contents

Introduction

In today's world, we often shield our tender hearts from anything that might cause pain. Yet, our hearts are the vessels of the most potent emotion: LOVE—literally "energy in motion." With LOVE, all things become possible through the divine power bestowed upon us by our Creator. What a magnificent gift!

This book is a journey of devotion, designed to help you take time each day to nurture yourself. It's crafted to inspire positivity and to encourage choosing love over fear, healing your own heart and the hearts of others. Discover the overwhelming power of LOVE that resides within you.

Learn to harness this wonderful gift of love in both grand and simple ways throughout your daily life. When you give love to yourself and to others, you also receive this same love back, enriched by God's universal love energy.

"Keep on asking, and it will be given to you; keep on seeking, and you will find; keep on knocking, and it will be opened to you. For everyone asking receives; everyone seeking finds; and to everyone knocking, it will be opened." — Matthew 7:7-8

I encourage you to use the power of love to connect with your heavenly Father by cultivating the fruits of God's Love:

"But the fruit of the Spirit is love, joy, peace, forbearance, kindness, goodness, faithfulness, gentleness, and self-control. Against such things, there is no law." — Galatians 5:22-23

"There is no fear in love, but perfect love throws fear outside....as for us we love because he first loved us."

 1 John 4:18,19

"God is love." — 1 John 4:8

Your journey begins right where you are. My hope is for you to experience a year filled with all the enriching blessings that Love can bring. Remember, "It is more blessed to give than to receive" (Acts 20:35)—the secret lies in the giving of love.

Start this book on any day and in any season—it's designed to flow with the rhythm of life, moving with the cycles of the earth, moon, and stars.

This book is inclusive and non-denominational, welcoming all spiritually-minded individuals open to exploring new ways to connect with our universal creator using the power of love that inherently resides within each of us. Everyone has the capacity to love; it is our divine right.

Chapter 1: Winter
Reflection and Inner Peace

Winter is a season of stillness and introspection, where the world seems to slow down, blanketed in quiet and calm. This time of year, naturally invites us to turn inward, reflect on our journey, and seek inner peace amidst the external cold.

December marks the beginning of this inward journey, where we focus on cultivating the inner light that guides us through the darkest days. As the days grow shorter and the nights longer, the gift of presence becomes a vital tool for maintaining our inner light. This month, you are invited to embrace the present moment fully, reflect on the past year's journey, and set intentions for the future.

As we enter January, the focus shifts to nurturing the soul, an essential practice for maintaining inner peace and resilience. January, with its fresh start and new beginnings, offers a time to cultivate inner stillness and reflect on personal growth. It's a month for honoring the resilience and strength you have built over time, while also nourishing yourself with compassion and care. The coldness of winter contrasts with the warmth of love, reminding us that joy and contentment are not dependent on external circumstances but are found within.

February, the final month of winter, focuses on embracing self-love as a powerful force for inner peace. This is a time to celebrate love in all its forms—romantic, platonic, and most importantly, the love you have for yourself. As the world around you begin to show early signs of spring, you are encouraged to nurture connections with loved ones, embrace self-acceptance, and radiate love and compassion. Love is not only the foundation of peace but also a transformative force that can heal and uplift. By the end of February, as the days start to lengthen, you will have laid a strong foundation of self-love and peace, ready to blossom as the world awakens in spring.

In this chapter, as you journey through the winter months, you will explore the profound connection between love and inner peace. Each devotion is designed to guide you through a season of reflection and growth, helping you to cultivate a deeper sense of love and tranquility within, no matter the challenges you may face.

December: Embracing the Gift of Presence

December brings with it the festive spirit of connection and celebration, a time when we are encouraged to embrace the true gift of presence—both within ourselves and in our relationships with others. This is a month rich with opportunities to savor the moments that make up our lives, to be fully present in the connections, traditions, and quiet joys that the holiday season brings. As the year draws to a close, we are invited to reflect on our relationships and the profound impact of simply being there—fully and wholeheartedly—for both our loved ones and ourselves.

This chapter is a heart-to-heart invitation to explore the power of presence as a source of warmth, comfort, and joy during the colder days. Through thoughtful practices and daily reflections, you will cultivate a deeper awareness of the present moment, enhancing your capacity for mindfulness and gratitude. Each devotion is lovingly crafted to draw you closer to the heart of what truly matters—connecting authentically with those around you, appreciating the beauty of the season, and finding peace in the here and now.

Week 1: Embracing the Gift of Presence

The holiday season, with its flurry of activities and gatherings, can easily become overwhelming. Yet, within this busyness lies a profound opportunity to practice presence—being fully aware and engaged in each moment. Embracing the gift of presence allows us to truly savor the joys of the season, from the twinkling lights to the laughter of loved ones. It's about being mindful of our experiences and the emotions they evoke, ensuring that we are not just going through the motions, but are truly living and experiencing the depth of each moment.

December 1st: Mindful Morning Ritual

Starting your day with intention sets the tone for the hours to come. Instead of jumping out of bed and rushing into your day, take a moment to embrace the quiet of the morning and be fully present.

Begin your day with a mindful morning ritual. Before you even get out of bed, take a few deep breaths and bring your attention to the sensations of your body and the rhythm of your breath. As you move through your morning routine—whether it's making your bed, brewing coffee, or brushing your teeth—do each task slowly and mindfully. Focus on the sensory details: the warmth of the mug in your hands, the aroma of your coffee, the feel of the water on your skin. Allow these moments to ground you in the present.

Words of Wisdom: "Mindfulness is the art of being fully awake in the present moment." —Thich Nhat Hanh

From the Bible: "This is the day that Jehovah has made; let us rejoice and be glad in it." —Psalm 118:24

Reflection Question: How does starting your day with mindfulness affect your ability to stay present throughout the day?

December 2nd: Being Present with Loved Ones

The holiday season is a time for connection, but often, we're physically present with our loved ones while our minds are elsewhere. Today, focus on truly being present with those you care about, giving them your full attention.

Spend quality time with a loved one today—whether it's a partner, child, friend, or family member. Turn off your phone, avoid distractions, and dedicate this time solely to them. Engage in an activity you both enjoy, such as cooking a meal together, playing a game, or simply having a deep conversation. Listen actively, make eye contact, and be fully engaged in the moment. This presence will strengthen your bond and create meaningful memories.

Words of Wisdom: "The greatest gift you can give someone is your presence." —Thich Nhat Hanh

From the Bible: "Love one another with brotherly affection. Outdo one another in showing honor." —Romans 12:10

Reflection Question: How does being fully present with your loved ones enhance your relationships?

December 3rd: Savoring the Simple Moments

In the midst of holiday preparations, it's easy to overlook the simple, everyday moments that bring joy and contentment. Today, make an effort to slow down and savor these moments, allowing them to fill you with peace and gratitude.

Choose a simple activity that you often rush through—like eating a meal, drinking a cup of tea, or taking a walk—and do it mindfully. For example, if you're having a meal, pay attention to the colors, textures, and flavors of the food. Eat slowly, savoring each bite, and notice how it nourishes your body. By bringing mindfulness to these ordinary moments, you'll find greater enjoyment and presence in your daily life.

Words of Wisdom: "When you savor a moment, it becomes more than just a memory; it becomes a part of who you are." —Pema Chodron, *Comfortable with Uncertainty*

From the Bible: "For everything there is an appointed time, even a time for every affair under the heavens." —Ecclesiastes 3:1

Reflection Question: What simple moments can you savor today, and how does this practice help you stay grounded in the present?

December 4th: Practicing Gratitude for the Present Moment

Gratitude is a powerful tool for bringing you into the present. By focusing on what you're thankful for right now, you can shift your attention away from worries and distractions, anchoring yourself in the here and now.

Throughout the day, take time to pause and mentally note three things you're grateful for in that exact moment. It could be the warmth of the sun on your face, the sound of laughter, or the feeling of being surrounded by loved ones. You can also keep a small notebook with you and jot down these moments of gratitude as they arise. By the end of the day, review your list and reflect on how these moments made you feel more present and connected.

Words of Wisdom: "Gratitude is the heart's memory." —Rhonda Byrne, *The Power*

From the Bible: "Always rejoice. Pray constantly. Give thanks for everything." —1 Thessalonians 5:16-18

Reflection Question: How does practicing gratitude help you stay present and appreciate the current moment more fully?

December 5th: The Gift of Compassion

As December unfolds, the demands of the season can sometimes leave us feeling stretched thin. For many of us—whether we are single mothers juggling work and home, mothers nurturing our families, or women striving to meet the expectations of society—the pressure can be immense. In these moments, it is essential to remember the power of compassion, not just for others, but for ourselves.

Compassion begins within. Often, we extend kindness and understanding to those around us but forget to offer the same grace to ourselves. Today, take a moment to practice self-compassion. Acknowledge the challenges you face and the strength it takes to meet them. Recognize that it's okay to feel tired, to need a break, or to not have all the answers. Embrace the imperfections that make you human.

As you cultivate compassion for yourself, you'll find it easier to extend that same warmth to others. This could mean offering a listening ear to a friend who is struggling, helping a neighbor in need, or simply being patient with your children when they test your limits. Compassion is a gift that grows the more it is given, creating a ripple effect of love and understanding in your home, your community, and the world.

Words of Wisdom: "Compassion is not a relationship between the healer and the wounded. It's a relationship between equals." —Pema Chodron, *Comfortable with Uncertainty*

From the Bible: "Just as you want men to do to you, do the same way to them." —Luke 6:31

Reflection Question: How can you practice compassion towards yourself today, and how can that self-compassion overflow into your interactions with others?

December 6th: The Power of Forgiveness

As we continue through December, the holiday season often brings to mind memories of past hurts and unresolved conflicts. Whether it's a strained relationship with a family member, lingering resentment from an old friendship, or even disappointment in yourself, these emotions can weigh heavily on your heart. Today, let's explore the transformative power of forgiveness.

Forgiveness is a gift you give to yourself. It doesn't mean that you excuse the hurt or forget the pain, but it frees you from the burden of carrying it. Holding onto anger and resentment only drains your energy and steals your peace. By choosing to forgive, you release yourself from the grip of the past and make room for healing and renewal.

Take a moment to think about someone you need to forgive—perhaps it's even yourself. Offer that person or yourself a silent blessing, asking for peace and understanding. Remember, forgiveness is a process; it's okay if it takes time. Each step you take toward forgiveness brings you closer to inner freedom.

Words of Wisdom: "Forgiveness does not change the past, but it does enlarge the future." —Paul Boese

From the Bible: "And whenever you stand praying, forgive, if you have anything against anyone, so that your Father in the heavens may also forgive you your trespasses." —Mark 11:25

Reflection Question: Who or what do you need to forgive today? How can releasing this burden bring you peace and freedom?

December 7th: Nurturing Gratitude

The holiday season often reminds us of the many blessings in our lives, but it's easy to overlook these when we're caught up in the rush of daily life. Gratitude is a powerful practice that shifts our focus from what we lack to the abundance that already surrounds us. Today, let's nurture a heart of gratitude.

Gratitude is a magnet for miracles. When we express genuine thanks for the small and large blessings in our lives, we align ourselves with the flow of abundance. This doesn't mean ignoring life's challenges, but rather choosing to see the good in the midst of it. Start your day by writing down three things you are grateful for, no matter how simple they may seem. It could be the warmth of your morning coffee, a kind word from a friend, or the roof over your head.

As you go through your day, continue to notice and appreciate the blessings around you. Gratitude turns what we have into enough, and often more than enough. It fills our hearts with contentment and opens the door to greater joy and fulfillment.

Words of Wisdom: "The more grateful you are, the more you attract things to be grateful for." —Rhonda Byrne, *The Power*

From the Bible: "I will give thanks to Jehovah with all my heart; I will tell of all your wonderful works." —Psalm 9:1

Reflection Question: How can you incorporate a daily gratitude practice into your life, and what blessings are you especially thankful for today?

Week 2: Reflecting on the Year's Journey

As we move into the second week of December, the holiday season provides a natural pause, inviting us to look back on the year that has passed. This is a time to reflect on the journey we've taken—both the triumphs and the challenges. It's an opportunity to acknowledge our growth, celebrate our successes, and learn from our experiences.

December 8th: Honoring Your Growth

This past year has likely been filled with moments of both joy and difficulty, each contributing to the person you are today. It's easy to focus on what didn't go as planned, but today, let's shift our attention to how much you've grown. Consider the ways you've evolved—whether it's becoming more patient, resilient, or compassionate.

Take a moment to honor your growth. Reflect on the challenges you've overcome and the strength you've gained from those experiences. Remember, growth often happens in the quiet moments when we persevere despite the odds. You are stronger than you were a year ago, and that is something to be proud of.

Words of Wisdom: "You grow through what you go through." — Wayne Dyer, *There's a Spiritual Solution to Every Problem*

From the Bible: "You have guided me with your advice, and afterward you will lead me to glory." —Psalm 73:24

Reflection Question: In what areas of your life have you grown the most this year, and how can you continue to nurture that growth?

December 9th: Learning from Challenges

Reflecting on the past year inevitably brings to mind the challenges we've faced. Whether they were big or small, these difficulties have shaped us in profound ways. Today, let's take a moment to consider what these challenges have taught us.

Every challenge carries a lesson. It might have taught you about patience, courage, or the importance of setting boundaries. Perhaps it revealed something about your own strength or the value of the support system around you. Acknowledge these lessons, even if they came through pain or struggle. They are part of the journey that has made you who you are.

Words of Wisdom: "Every adversity, every failure, every heartache carries with it the seed of an equal or greater benefit." —Napoleon Hill

From the Bible: "Consider it all joy, my brothers, when you meet with various trials, knowing as you do that this tested quality of your faith produces endurance." —James 1:2-3

Reflection Question: What challenges have you faced this year, and what valuable lessons have you learned from them?

December 10th: Celebrating Successes

Amidst the challenges, it's equally important to celebrate your successes—big and small. These victories, whether in your personal life, career, or relationships, are milestones of your journey. Today, take time to acknowledge and celebrate your achievements.

Success comes in many forms. It could be reaching a career goal, strengthening a relationship, or simply making it through a tough day. Each success, no matter how small, deserves recognition. Celebrate your wins and allow yourself to feel proud of what you've accomplished this year.

Words of Wisdom: "Celebrate your successes, no matter how small, for they are the building blocks of your future." —Rhonda Byrne, *The Power*

From the Bible: "Jehovah will make you prosper in all your work and in all that you undertake." —Deuteronomy 30:9

Reflection Question: What are some of the successes you've experienced this year, and how can you celebrate them today?

December 11th: Embracing Change

The end of the year often brings with it a sense of change—some of it welcomed, and some of it unexpected. Change can be difficult, but it is also a powerful catalyst for growth. Today, let's reflect on the changes you've experienced and how they have shaped your life.

Change is a natural part of life. It can be a doorway to new opportunities, a chance to start fresh, or an invitation to let go of what no longer serves you. Embrace the changes you've encountered this year, knowing that each one has contributed to your personal evolution.

Words of Wisdom: "Change is inevitable, growth is optional." —John Maxwell

From the Bible: "Trust in Jehovah and do good; Reside in the earth, and act with faithfulness." —Psalm 37:3

Reflection Question: What changes have you experienced this year, and how have they helped you grow?

December 12th: Finding Inner Peace

As you reflect on the year, it's important to find moments of peace amidst the busyness of life. Inner peace is not the absence of challenges but the ability to remain calm and centered despite them. Today, focus on cultivating this peace within yourself.

Inner peace is a sanctuary. It's a place you can return to when life feels overwhelming. This peace comes from trusting in the process of life, knowing that everything unfolds as it should. Take time today to meditate, pray, or simply sit in silence, allowing peace to fill your heart.

Words of Wisdom: "Peace comes from within. Do not seek it without." —Buddha

From the Bible: "You will keep in perfect peace those whose minds are steadfast, because they trust in you." —Isaiah 26:3

Reflection Question: How can you create more moments of inner peace in your daily life, especially during challenging times?

December 13th: Gratitude for the Journey

As this week of reflection comes to a close, take a moment to express gratitude for the journey you've been on this year. Every step, every challenge, every joy has brought you to this point. Gratitude is a powerful force that can transform your outlook and fill your heart with contentment.

Gratitude is the foundation of a joyful life. It shifts your focus from what's missing to the abundance that surrounds you. Today, take time to thank yourself for your perseverance, thank the people who have supported you, and thank the universe for guiding you through another year.

Words of Wisdom: "Gratitude is the completion of thankfulness. Thankfulness may consist merely of words. Gratitude is shown in acts." —David O. McKay

From the Bible: "Give thanks always for everything to our God and Father in the name of our Lord Jesus Christ." —Ephesians 5:20

Reflection Question: What are you most grateful for as you reflect on this past year, and how can you carry that gratitude into the new year?

December 14th: Setting Intentions for the New Year

As the year draws closer to an end, it's a powerful time to start thinking about the future and the intentions you want to set for the coming year. Setting intentions is more than just making resolutions; it's about aligning your actions with your deepest desires and values, creating a life that reflects who you truly are.

Intentions are seeds for your future. They are the thoughts and desires you plant now that will grow and blossom in the months to come. Take time today to reflect on what you want to manifest in your life. What are your hopes and dreams for the new year? What qualities do you want to cultivate? What goals do you want to achieve?

Spend a few quiet moments writing down your intentions for the new year. Be clear and specific, but also be gentle with yourself. These intentions are not about perfection but about progress and growth. As you set these intentions, visualize them taking root and growing, bringing positive change into your life.

Words of Wisdom: "Intention is the starting point of every dream— the seed of creation." —Deepak Chopra

From the Bible: "Commit to Jehovah whatever you do, and he will establish your plans." —Proverbs 16:3

Reflection Question: What are your most important intentions for the new year, and how can you begin to nurture these intentions starting today?

Week 3: Nurturing Seeds of Intention

As we enter the third week of December, the focus shifts toward nurturing the seeds of intention that we've planted for the new year. This is a time for tending to these intentions with care, ensuring they are rooted in love, purpose, and authenticity. For all women—whether single mothers, working professionals, or those balancing multiple roles—this week is about preparing the soil of your life so that your intentions can grow strong and true.

December 15th: Cultivating Patience

As you begin to nurture your intentions for the new year, it's important to remember that growth takes time. Patience is a vital part of the process. Whether you're working toward personal goals, caring for your family, or managing the demands of everyday life, it's easy to feel frustrated when progress seems slow. But just like a seed that takes time to sprout, your intentions need time to develop.

Patience is an act of faith. It's trusting that the work you're doing today will bear fruit in the future. As you care for your intentions, be gentle with yourself. Recognize that growth doesn't happen overnight, and that's okay. Each step you take, no matter how small, is moving you closer to your goals.

Words of Wisdom: "Patience is not the ability to wait, but the ability to keep a good attitude while waiting." —Joyce Meyer

From the Bible: "But let patience complete its work, so that you may be complete and sound in all respects, not lacking in anything." —James 1:4

Reflection Question: In what areas of your life do you need to cultivate more patience, and how can embracing patience help your intentions to grow?

December 16th: Embracing Flexibility

As women, we often set high expectations for ourselves and those around us. However, life rarely goes exactly as planned. Embracing flexibility allows you to adapt to the changes and challenges that arise, without losing sight of your intentions. Whether you're a single mother balancing work and home, or a woman striving to meet her personal goals, flexibility is key to navigating life's twists and turns.

Flexibility is the strength to bend without breaking. It's about adjusting your course when necessary, while keeping your eyes on the bigger picture. Today, consider how you can bring more flexibility into your life. This might mean letting go of rigid expectations, being open to new approaches, or simply allowing yourself to go with the flow when plans change.

Words of Wisdom: "Blessed are the flexible, for they shall not be bent out of shape." —Michael Beckwith

From the Bible: "By your endurance you will preserve your lives." — Luke 21:19

Reflection Question: How can embracing flexibility help you maintain balance in your life while nurturing your intentions?

December 17th: Nourishing Yourself

As you nurture your intentions, it's essential not to forget to nourish yourself. As women, we often prioritize the needs of others—our children, partners, families, and communities—sometimes to the detriment of our own well-being. But just as a gardener must care for herself to tend her garden, you must care for your body, mind, and spirit to fully nurture your intentions.

Self-care is not a luxury; it's a necessity. Take time today to do something that replenishes your energy and uplifts your spirit. This could be as simple as taking a quiet walk, enjoying a favorite hobby, or spending time in prayer or meditation. By nourishing yourself, you ensure that you have the strength and clarity needed to continue nurturing your intentions.

Words of Wisdom: "When you take care of yourself, you're taking care of the universe." —Lynne McTaggart, *Living the Field*

From the Bible: "And the second, like it, is this: 'You must love your neighbor as yourself.'" —Mark 12:31

Reflection Question: What is one self-care practice you can incorporate into your routine to ensure you are nourished and energized to pursue your intentions?

December 18th: Trusting the Process

When you plant a seed, you cannot see the roots that are forming beneath the surface. Similarly, when you set an intention, much of the growth happens in ways that are not immediately visible. Trusting the process means believing in the unseen progress that is happening in your life, even when the results are not yet apparent.

Trust is the foundation of faith. It's knowing that your efforts are not in vain, and that the universe is working in your favor. Today, focus on releasing any doubts or fears that may be holding you back. Trust that as you continue to nurture your intentions with love and patience, they will manifest in their own time.

Words of Wisdom: "Trust the process. Your time is coming. Just do the work and the results will handle themselves." —Tony Gaskins

From the Bible: "Faith is the assured expectation of what is hoped for, the evident demonstration of realities that are not seen." —Hebrews 11:1

Reflection Question: How can you cultivate greater trust in the process of nurturing your intentions, even when you can't see immediate results?

December 19th: Letting Go of Perfection

Perfectionism can be a heavy burden, especially for women who strive to be everything to everyone. Whether you're a mother, a professional, or someone trying to meet personal goals, the pressure to be perfect can stifle your growth and hinder your progress. Today, let's focus on letting go of perfection and embracing the beauty of imperfection.

Perfection is not the goal; progress is. Allow yourself the grace to make mistakes, to learn, and to grow. Remember that your worth is not determined by flawless execution, but by your commitment to your journey. Letting go of perfection frees you to be more present, more joyful, and more authentic in your life.

Words of Wisdom: "Perfectionism is a dream killer, because it's just fear disguised as trying to do your best." —Elizabeth Gilbert

From the Bible: "But he said to me: 'My undeserved kindness is sufficient for you, for my power is being made perfect in weakness.'" —2 Corinthians 12:9

Reflection Question: How can releasing the need for perfection help you to be more compassionate with yourself and others as you nurture your intentions?

December 20th: Reaffirming Your Intentions

As we near the end of the year, it's important to take a moment to reaffirm the intentions you've set. Reaffirming your intentions means reconnecting with the reasons why you set them in the first place. It's about reminding yourself of your goals, your purpose, and your commitment to making them a reality.

Reaffirmation strengthens your resolve. Today, spend some time in quiet reflection, revisiting the intentions you've planted. Visualize them growing and thriving in the new year. Speak your intentions out loud, write them down again, or create a vision board that represents them. By

---

reaffirming your intentions, you strengthen your commitment to seeing them through.

Words of Wisdom: "When you are clear about your intentions, the universe conspires to make it happen." —Sadhguru, *Inner Engineering*

From the Bible: "For I well know the thoughts that I am thinking toward you, declares Jehovah, thoughts of peace and not of calamity, to give you a future and a hope." —Jeremiah 29:11

Reflection Question: How can you reaffirm your intentions today in a way that reignites your passion and commitment to them?

December 21st: Embracing the Winter Solstice – Illuminating Your Inner Light

Today marks the Winter Solstice, the shortest day and longest night of the year. For many, this time symbolizes the darkness that can sometimes envelop our lives, but it also serves as a powerful reminder that even in the darkest times, there is always light waiting to emerge. The solstice is a turning point—a moment to reflect on the past year and to look forward to the light and possibilities that lie ahead.

Illuminating your inner light is a profound act of self-love. As women, we often find ourselves nurturing others, providing light and warmth for those around us. But today, on this sacred day of the solstice, let's turn inward and focus on the light that resides within each of us. This light is your spirit, your essence, your strength—it's the part of you that remains unshaken by the storms of life.

Take a moment today to connect with your inner light. You might light a candle as a physical representation of this light, or spend time in meditation, visualizing a warm, glowing light within your heart. Let this light guide you through any darkness you may be facing. Trust that this light will grow stronger as the days begin to lengthen, bringing new opportunities, hope, and growth.

Words of Wisdom: "The darkness is not an absence of light. It is an invitation to find your light within." —Dr. Joe Dispenza, *Becoming Supernatural*

From the Bible: "Jehovah is my light and my salvation. Whom shall I fear? Jehovah is the stronghold of my life. Whom shall I dread?" —Psalm 27:1

Reflection Question: How can you nurture and embrace your inner light during this time of year, and how can it guide you as you move forward into the new year?

Week 4: Illuminating with Inner Wisdom

As we enter the final week of December, the year draws to a close, and the focus shifts to the wisdom we have gained. This week is about embracing and illuminating the inner wisdom that has been cultivated through your experiences, your challenges, and your triumphs. It's about recognizing that within you lies a wellspring of knowledge and understanding that can guide you into the new year with clarity and confidence. This wisdom is not only the result of your personal journey but also a reflection of the collective experiences of women everywhere. Let's explore how to tap into and share this inner wisdom, allowing it to light the way forward.

December 22nd: Trusting Your Inner Voice

Throughout life, there are countless voices—external opinions, societal expectations, and well-meaning advice—that can drown out the most important voice of all: your own. Today, let's focus on trusting your inner voice, that quiet, steady whisper within that knows what is truly best for you.

Your inner voice is your truest guide. It's the part of you that speaks from a place of love and deep understanding. To hear it, you may need to tune out the noise of the world and spend some quiet time in reflection or meditation. Trust that your inner voice has your best interests at heart, guiding you toward choices that align with your authentic self.

Words of Wisdom: "The soul always knows what to do to heal itself. The challenge is to silence the mind." —Caroline Myss

From the Bible: "The one walking with the wise will become wise, but the one who has dealings with the stupid will fare badly." —Proverbs 13:20

Reflection Question: How can you create more space in your life to listen to and trust your inner voice?

December 23rd: Sharing Your Wisdom

Wisdom is not meant to be hoarded; it's a gift that grows when shared with others. As women, we have the unique ability to connect deeply with those around us, offering support, guidance, and insights drawn from our own experiences. Today, let's focus on how you can share your inner wisdom with others in meaningful ways.

Sharing wisdom is an act of love. Whether it's offering advice to a friend, mentoring someone who is struggling, or simply being a compassionate listener, your wisdom has the power to uplift and inspire others. Reflect on the lessons you've learned this year and consider how you can use them to help those around you.

Words of Wisdom: "When you learn, teach. When you get, give." — Maya Angelou

From the Bible: "A word spoken at the right time is as beautiful as golden apples in a silver bowl." —Proverbs 25:11

Reflection Question: What wisdom have you gained this year that you can share with someone in need of encouragement or guidance?

December 24th: Embracing the Wisdom of the Past

As we prepare to transition into a new year, it's important to reflect on the wisdom that has been handed down to us through generations—whether from our mothers, grandmothers, or the countless women who have walked this path before us. Today, let's embrace the wisdom of the past and honor the legacy of strength and resilience that has been passed down to you.

The wisdom of the past is a foundation for the future. Think about the lessons and values that have been instilled in you by the women who came before you. How have these teachings shaped who you are today? By acknowledging and embracing this inherited wisdom, you carry forward the strength and guidance of your ancestors into the new year.

Words of Wisdom: "We are each a composite of the women who came before us, their struggles and triumphs written into our very DNA." — Lynne McTaggart, *Living the Field*

From the Bible: "Remember the days of old; consider the years of past generations. Ask your father, and he can tell you; your elders, and they will inform you." —Deuteronomy 32:7

Reflection Question: How can you honor the wisdom passed down to you, and how will you carry it forward into the new year?

December 25th: The Gift of Inner Peace

Today, as the world celebrates a day of peace and goodwill, it's an opportune moment to focus on the gift of inner peace. Inner peace is the calm and serenity that comes from knowing that, no matter what is happening around you, you are grounded in your own wisdom and truth.

Inner peace is the most precious gift you can give yourself. It's the foundation upon which all other aspects of your life are built. Take time today to nurture this peace within yourself. Whether through prayer, meditation, or simply enjoying a quiet moment, allow this peace to wash over you, filling your heart and mind with tranquility.

Words of Wisdom: "Peace is not something you wish for; it's something you make, something you do, something you are, and something you give away." —John Lennon

From the Bible: "Let the peace of the Christ rule in your hearts, for you were called to that peace in one body. And show yourselves thankful." —Colossians 3:15

Reflection Question: What practices can you incorporate into your life to cultivate and maintain inner peace, even in challenging times?

December 26th: Illuminating Your Path Forward

As the year comes to an end, it's a time to look ahead and illuminate the path forward with the wisdom you've gained. This is a moment to set your sights on the future, carrying with you the lessons, insights, and growth that have shaped your journey thus far.

Your path forward is illuminated by the light of your wisdom. Reflect on the ways in which you have grown this year and how that growth will guide you into the new year. Consider the intentions you've set and how you will continue to nurture them as you move forward. Trust that the wisdom you've gained will lead you to new opportunities and greater fulfillment.

Words of Wisdom: "The best way to predict the future is to create it." —Abraham Lincoln

From the Bible: "Your word is a lamp to my foot, and a light for my path." —Psalm 119:105

Reflection Question: How can you use the wisdom and insights you've gained this year to illuminate your path into the new year?

December 27th: Reflecting on Your Spiritual Journey

As the year comes to a close, it's a meaningful time to reflect on your spiritual journey. This journey is unique for every woman—whether you find strength in your faith, wisdom in the universe, or peace in nature. Today, let's take a moment to honor the spiritual growth you've experienced and the ways in which your connection to the divine has deepened.

Your spiritual journey is a testament to your resilience and faith. Reflect on the ways you've drawn closer to your spiritual center this year. How has your relationship with the divine, with the universe, or with your inner self evolved? Celebrate the moments of insight, the times of solace, and the growth that has come from seeking and finding spiritual truth.

Words of Wisdom: "The spiritual journey is the unlearning of fear and the acceptance of love." —Marianne Williamson

From the Bible: "Draw close to God, and he will draw close to you." —James 4:8

Reflection Question: How has your spiritual journey evolved this year, and what practices can you continue or start to deepen your spiritual connection in the coming year?

December 28th: The Power of Surrender

There are moments in life when we must surrender—let go of the need to control every outcome and trust that everything will unfold as it's meant to. Surrendering is not a sign of weakness but of profound strength and faith. Today, let's focus on the power of surrender.

Surrender is an act of trust. It's about releasing the weight of expectations and allowing the universe, God, or whatever higher power you believe in, to guide your path. By surrendering, you open yourself up to possibilities you may not have imagined, and you allow grace to flow into your life.

Words of Wisdom: "When you let go of the need for control, you create space for the miraculous." —Michael Singer, *The Untethered Soul*

From the Bible: "Trust in Jehovah with all your heart, and do not rely on your own understanding." —Proverbs 3:5

Reflection Question: What areas of your life would benefit from surrendering control, and how can this act of surrender bring more peace and flow into your life?

December 29th: Embracing New Beginnings

As we approach the end of the year, it's natural to think about the fresh start that the new year offers. New beginnings are full of promise and potential, but they also require us to release the past and embrace what's to come. Today, let's focus on the excitement and hope that new beginnings bring.

Every ending is a new beginning. As you prepare to step into the new year, consider what you need to let go of to fully embrace this fresh start. Whether it's an old habit, a lingering resentment, or a limiting belief, releasing these will make room for the new and wonderful things that await you.

Words of Wisdom: "The secret to change is to focus all of your energy not on fighting the old, but on building the new." —Socrates

From the Bible: "Look! I am making all things new." —Revelation 21:5

Reflection Question: What do you need to release as you prepare for the new year, and how can you embrace the new beginnings that are on the horizon?

December 30th: Gratitude for the Past Year

Before the year closes, it's important to take a moment to express gratitude for all that the past year has brought—both the joys and the

---

challenges. Gratitude is a powerful force that can transform our perspective, helping us to see the blessings in every experience.

Gratitude turns what we have into enough. Reflect on the moments that have made this year special—the relationships you've deepened, the goals you've achieved, the lessons you've learned. Even the difficult times have shaped you into the person you are today. Take a few moments to give thanks for all of it, knowing that each experience has been a stepping stone on your journey.

Words of Wisdom: "Gratitude makes sense of our past, brings peace for today, and creates a vision for tomorrow." —Melody Beattie

From the Bible: "Give thanks to Jehovah, for he is good; his loyal love endures forever." —Psalm 107:1

Reflection Question: What are you most grateful for as you reflect on the past year, and how can you carry this gratitude into the new year?

December 31st: Stepping into the New Year with Confidence

As the final day of the year arrives, it's time to look ahead with hope and confidence. The new year is a blank canvas, ready to be filled with your dreams, goals, and intentions. Today, let's focus on stepping into the new year with a sense of inspiration and trust in yourself.

You have everything you need to create the life you desire. The experiences of this past year have prepared you for the journey ahead. As you step into the new year, carry with you the wisdom you've gained, the strength you've built, and the love that surrounds you. Trust in your ability to navigate whatever comes your way with grace and courage.

Words of Wisdom: "You are never too old to set another goal or to dream a new dream." —C.S. Lewis

From the Bible: "For I know the thoughts that I am thinking toward you, declares Jehovah, thoughts of peace and not of calamity, to give you a future and a hope." —Jeremiah 29:11

Reflection Question: As you step into the new year, what intentions and goals will you carry with you, and how can you approach them with confidence and trust in yourself?

January: Nurturing the Soul

As the new year dawns, January presents a unique opportunity to turn inward and focus on nurturing the soul. The beginning of the year is often filled with resolutions and goals, but before diving into the external pursuits, it's essential to take time to care for the inner self. January is a month of quiet reflection, an invitation to cultivate inner peace and reconnect with the core of who you are.

The winter season, with its cold and stillness, mirrors the journey inward that this month encourages. Just as the earth rests beneath a blanket of snow, gathering strength for the coming spring, you too can use this time to restore your spirit, find clarity, and build a strong foundation for the year ahead. This is a season to nurture your soul, to honor the wisdom you've gained, and to embrace the quiet power that lies within you.

For women—whether you are a single mother balancing countless responsibilities, a working professional navigating the demands of career and home, or simply someone seeking deeper meaning—January is your time. It's a time to cultivate inner stillness, reflect on personal growth, honor your resilience, and nourish yourself with self-compassion. This month is not just about setting new goals, but about honoring the journey you've already traveled and preparing your spirit for what's to come.

Each week in January will guide you through a different aspect of soul nurturing, helping you to center yourself, reflect on your progress, and build the resilience and strength needed to thrive in the year ahead. As you embark on this journey, remember that nurturing the soul is not a one-time task, but a lifelong commitment to yourself, one that will bring joy, peace, and fulfillment to every aspect of your life.

Week 1: Cultivating Inner Stillness

The start of the new year is often accompanied by a flurry of activity—planning, setting goals, and jumping into new routines. But before the

---

rush begins, it's essential to create space for inner stillness. This week is dedicated to cultivating that quiet center within you, where peace and clarity reside. Inner stillness is not about withdrawing from life but about finding a calm, unshakable foundation amid the busyness.

For many women, the demands of life—whether caring for family, managing a career, or navigating personal challenges—can make it difficult to find moments of peace. Yet, it is in these moments of stillness that we reconnect with our true selves, gain perspective, and recharge our spirits. This week, focus on creating small pockets of quiet in your day, whether through meditation, prayer, or simply sitting in silence.

Allow yourself to breathe deeply and let go of any tension or stress. As you cultivate inner stillness, you'll find that it becomes a source of strength, guiding you through the challenges and opportunities of the new year with grace and confidence. Remember, stillness is a powerful tool for nurturing the soul, providing the clarity needed to move forward with purpose.

January 1st: Finding Joy in Family Traditions

As we begin the new year, there's no better time to find joy in the simple yet meaningful traditions that connect us with our loved ones. Whether it's a family game night, cooking a special meal together, or cozying up for a movie marathon, these moments create lasting memories and strengthen the bonds we share. For single mothers, working women, or anyone balancing the demands of life, these traditions offer a chance to pause, laugh, and simply be present with those who matter most.

Creating these joyful moments is a way to nurture your soul and the souls of those you love. It's in these small, shared experiences that we find the deepest happiness, a contentment that transcends the busyness of our daily lives.

Words of Wisdom: "Happiness lies in the joy of achievement and the thrill of creative effort." —Franklin D. Roosevelt

—

From the Bible: "This is the day that Jehovah has made! Let us be joyful and rejoice in it." —Psalm 118:24

Reflection Question: How can you incorporate joyful traditions into your family life this year to create lasting memories?

January 2nd: Embracing the Warmth of Friendship

The cold winter months can sometimes bring a sense of isolation, but they also provide a perfect opportunity to deepen connections with friends. Whether through a virtual hangout, a coffee date, or a simple phone call, these interactions remind us of the warmth that comes from true companionship. For women juggling various roles, friendships can be a lifeline, offering support, laughter, and encouragement.

Take time today to reach out to a friend. Celebrate the joy of friendship by sharing stories, supporting each other's goals, and simply enjoying the connection. Friendships, like all relationships, need nurturing, and in doing so, we find a profound sense of belonging and joy.

Words of Wisdom: Words of Wisdom: "True friendship is an act of love—a spiritual connection that transcends time and distance." — Michael Singer, The Untethered Soul

From the Bible: "A true friend shows love at all times and is a brother who is born for times of distress." —Proverbs 17:17

Reflection Question: How can you nurture your friendships this year to ensure they continue to grow and bring joy into your life?

January 3rd: Spreading Joy in Your Community

As we seek to cultivate inner stillness, one powerful way to do so is by spreading joy within our community. Volunteering, supporting local businesses, or simply sharing a kind word with a neighbor can bring immense satisfaction and peace. For women, particularly those balancing many responsibilities, finding time to engage with the community can feel challenging, but even small acts can have a significant impact.

Consider how you can contribute to the joy and well-being of those around you. Whether through a small donation, participating in a community event, or offering your time, these actions not only benefit others but also fill your own heart with a sense of purpose and connection.

Words of Wisdom: "Joy is a net of love by which you can catch souls." —Mother Teresa

From the Bible: "Let your light shine before men, so that they may see your fine works and give glory to your Father who is in the heavens." — Matthew 5:16

Reflection Question: What small act of kindness can you perform this week to spread joy in your community?

January 4th: Nurturing Yourself with Joy

Amidst the responsibilities of caring for others and contributing to your community, it's essential not to overlook the importance of nurturing yourself. Engaging in hobbies, practicing self-care, or setting goals for personal growth are all ways to cultivate joy within. For women who are often the caregivers and supporters of others, prioritizing self-care is not just important—it's necessary.

Take time today to do something that brings you joy. Whether it's reading a book, taking a walk, or simply enjoying a moment of peace, these activities rejuvenate your spirit and help you approach life with renewed energy and positivity.

Words of Wisdom: "Joy does not simply happen to us. We have to choose joy and keep choosing it every day." —Henri Nouwen

From the Bible: "For you, O Jehovah, have made me rejoice over your works; I shout joyfully over the works of your hands." —Psalm 92:4

Reflection Question: How can you incorporate more joy-filled activities into your daily routine to nurture your well-being?

January 5th: Celebrating Small Achievements

As the new year begins, it's easy to focus on big goals and overlook the small victories that pave the way. Whether it's completing a task, reaching a personal milestone, or simply making it through a challenging day, these small achievements deserve to be celebrated. For women managing busy lives—whether single mothers, professionals, or caregivers—recognizing these moments of success can bring a deep sense of satisfaction and joy.

Take a moment today to acknowledge and celebrate your small wins. Each step forward is a testament to your strength and resilience. By appreciating these moments, you build momentum and positivity that will carry you through the bigger challenges ahead.

Words of Wisdom: "Every action, no matter how small, brings you closer to the life you are meant to create." —Lynne McTaggart, *Living the Field*

From the Bible: "Do not despise these small beginnings, for Jehovah rejoices to see the work begin." —Zechariah 4:10

Reflection Question: What small achievement can you celebrate today, and how does it contribute to your overall growth and happiness?

January 6th: Creating Joyful Connections with Friends

The start of the new year is an ideal time to reconnect with friends and strengthen the bonds that bring joy and support into your life. Whether it's through a planned excursion, a spontaneous meet-up, or simply reaching out with a heartfelt message, these connections are vital for your emotional well-being. For many women, friendships offer a safe space to share, laugh, and find encouragement.

Today, focus on creating or deepening your connections with friends. Organize a coffee date, plan an outing, or simply make time for a meaningful conversation. These moments of connection are not just enjoyable—they are essential for maintaining a balanced and joyful life.

Words of Wisdom: "When we share, that is poetry in the prose of life." —Sigmund Freud

From the Bible: "Iron sharpens iron, so one man sharpens his friend." —Proverbs 27:17

Reflection Question: How can you make more room in your life for the friendships that bring you joy and support?

January 7th: Finding Joy in Nature's Embrace

Nature has a unique way of restoring our spirits, offering peace and joy that can be hard to find in our busy lives. Whether you're taking a walk in the park, breathing in the crisp winter air, or simply gazing at the beauty of a snow-covered landscape, these moments in nature can be profoundly healing. For women who are constantly giving of themselves—whether at home, at work, or in the community—nature provides a necessary retreat to recharge and reflect.

Spend some time in nature today, allowing it to rejuvenate your soul. Even a few moments outside can bring a sense of calm and joy, helping you to reconnect with yourself and the world around you.

Words of Wisdom: "Nature does not hurry, yet everything is accomplished." —Lao Tzu

From the Bible: "The heavens are declaring the glory of God; the skies proclaim the work of his hands." —Psalm 19:1

Reflection Question: How can you incorporate more time in nature into your routine, and how does being in nature bring joy and peace to your life?

Week 2: Reflecting on Personal Growth

As we move into the second week of January, the focus shifts from cultivating inner stillness to reflecting on the personal growth you've experienced over the past year. This is a time to look back on the challenges you've faced, the lessons you've learned, and the ways you've evolved as a person. For women in all walks of life—whether you are navigating the complexities of motherhood, building a career, or balancing both—acknowledging your growth is an essential step in nurturing your soul.

Personal growth is not always easy to see in the moment. It often occurs gradually, through small changes in how you think, feel, and respond to the world around you. This week is about recognizing and celebrating those changes, no matter how subtle they may be. Reflecting on your growth allows you to understand your journey more deeply and prepares you to continue evolving in the year ahead.

Each day this week will guide you through different aspects of personal growth, encouraging you to explore how far you've come and where you still want to go. You'll be invited to look at the challenges that have shaped you, the strengths you've developed, and the values that have guided you. By taking this time to reflect, you inspire yourself to move forward with a greater sense of purpose and confidence.

Remember, personal growth is a continuous process, one that requires patience, self-compassion, and an openness to learning. As you reflect this week, embrace the progress you've made, and trust that you are on the path to becoming the best version of yourself.

January 8th: Acknowledging Your Strengths

As you reflect on your personal growth, it's important to take a moment to acknowledge the strengths you've developed over the past year. Whether it's resilience in the face of challenges, the ability to remain calm under pressure, or the kindness you've shown to others, these strengths are the foundation of your growth. For many women, it's easy to overlook these qualities, focusing instead on what still needs improvement. But today, let's celebrate the strengths that have carried you through.

Recognizing your strengths is an act of self-love. These qualities are what make you unique and powerful. Write down the strengths you've noticed in yourself over the past year, and take pride in the person you're becoming.

Words of Wisdom: "The power to endure lies not in the body, but in the unwavering resilience of the soul." —Pema Chodron, *Comfortable with Uncertainty*

From the Bible: "Jehovah gives power to the tired one and full might to those lacking strength." —Isaiah 40:29

Reflection Question: What strengths have you developed over the past year, and how can they continue to support you in the year ahead?

January 9th: Learning from Your Challenges

Growth often comes from facing and overcoming challenges. These difficulties, though painful at the time, are opportunities for personal development. Whether you've dealt with loss, faced uncertainty, or navigated complex relationships, each challenge has taught you something valuable about yourself. Today, reflect on the lessons these challenges have brought.

Embrace the wisdom that comes from your struggles. Consider how these experiences have shaped your character, your perspectives, and your values. Understanding what you've learned from your challenges allows you to move forward with greater insight and resilience.

Words of Wisdom: "Out of difficulties grow miracles." —Jean de La Bruyère

From the Bible: "Happy is the man who keeps on enduring trial, because on becoming approved he will receive the crown of life, which Jehovah promised to those who continue loving him." —James 1:12

Reflection Question: What challenges have you faced this past year, and what valuable lessons have you learned from them?

January 10th: Celebrating Your Growth

Amidst the ups and downs of life, it's crucial to take time to celebrate your growth. Every step you've taken—whether forward or backward—has contributed to the person you are today. For many women, the demands of daily life can overshadow the progress you've made, but today is about honoring that progress. Recognize the courage, the effort, and the determination it has taken to grow.

Celebrate your growth, no matter how small it may seem. Reflect on the moments that have brought you joy, the goals you've achieved, and the ways you've expanded your horizons. This celebration is not just about what you've done, but about who you are becoming.

Words of Wisdom: "Growth is the only evidence of life." —John Henry Newman

From the Bible: "Jehovah your God will bless you in all the work of your hands, and you will lend to many nations but borrow from none." —Deuteronomy 15:6

Reflection Question: How can you celebrate your personal growth today, and what milestones are you most proud of?

January 11th: Embracing Change

Personal growth often requires embracing change—both the changes you've chosen and those that have been thrust upon you. Change can be unsettling, but it's also a catalyst for growth, pushing you out of your comfort zone and into new opportunities. As you reflect on the past year, consider the changes you've experienced and how they have contributed to your development.

Embrace change as a friend, not a foe. Recognize that each change, whether welcomed or resisted, has brought you closer to your true self. Trust that the changes you've gone through are leading you toward greater fulfillment and wisdom.

Words of Wisdom: "Change is the essence of life; be willing to surrender what you are for what you could become." —Reinhold Niebuhr

From the Bible: "The plans of the diligent surely lead to success, but all who are hasty surely head for poverty." —Proverbs 21:5

Reflection Question: What changes have you experienced this past year, and how have they contributed to your personal growth?

January 12th: Reflecting on the Power of Resilience

Resilience is the ability to bounce back from life's challenges, and it's a quality that women often embody without even realizing it. Over the past year, you've likely faced moments of doubt, stress, or hardship, yet here you are, continuing to move forward. Today, take time to reflect on your resilience—the quiet strength that has seen you through difficult times.

Recognize the power of your resilience. It's not about never falling down, but about getting back up each time with renewed determination. Your resilience is a testament to your inner strength and your commitment to keep going, no matter what.

Words of Wisdom: "Life doesn't get easier or more forgiving; we get stronger and more resilient." —Steve Maraboli

From the Bible: "Therefore we do not give up, but even if the man we are outside is wasting away, certainly the man we are inside is being renewed from day to day." —2 Corinthians 4:16

Reflection Question: How has your resilience helped you navigate the challenges of the past year, and how can you continue to strengthen this quality in your life?

January 13th: Understanding Your Growth Through Reflection

Reflection is a powerful tool for understanding your personal growth. By looking back on your experiences, you gain insights into your behaviors, choices, and the patterns that have shaped your life. For many women, reflection provides clarity and helps identify the areas where growth has occurred. Today, take time to reflect deeply on your journey.

Reflect on the lessons learned and the growth achieved. This process allows you to see the bigger picture of your life, helping you to appreciate the progress you've made and to plan for the future with wisdom and intention.

Words of Wisdom: "The unexamined life is not worth living." — Socrates

From the Bible: "Make me know your ways, O Jehovah; teach me your paths." —Psalm 25:4

Reflection Question: As you reflect on the past year, what patterns or lessons stand out to you, and how can you apply these insights to your future growth?

January 14th: Valuing the Journey of Growth

Personal growth is not just about reaching a destination; it's about valuing the journey itself. Each step you take, each experience you encounter, contributes to your ongoing development. For many women, the journey of growth is intertwined with the roles they play—whether as mothers, professionals, or individuals seeking fulfillment. Today, focus on valuing every part of your journey.

Embrace the journey with gratitude. Appreciate the highs and lows, the easy and hard days, as each has its own lessons and blessings. Recognizing the value in the journey helps you to stay present and fully engaged in your life.

Words of Wisdom: "It is good to have an end to journey toward, but it is the journey that matters in the end." —Ursula K. Le Guin

From the Bible: "I have come that they may have life and may have it in abundance." —John 10:10

Reflection Question: How can you find joy and gratitude in the journey of personal growth, appreciating each step for its unique contribution to your life?

Week 3: Honoring Resilience and Strength

As we step into the third week of January, the focus turns to honoring the resilience and strength that have carried you through life's challenges.

This week is about recognizing the inner fortitude that has helped you rise above adversity, navigate difficult situations, and continue moving forward with courage and determination. Resilience and strength are qualities that often go unnoticed, yet they are the bedrock of personal growth and fulfillment.

January 15th: Recognizing Your Inner Resilience

Resilience is a quiet force, often unnoticed until we look back and see how far we've come. It's the inner strength that carries us through the darkest times and helps us rise again after each fall. Today, take a moment to recognize the resilience within you—the power that has enabled you to keep moving forward despite challenges.

Resilience is the ability to adapt and thrive, not just survive. It's about transforming adversity into growth, using each setback as a stepping stone toward something greater. Reflect on the times you've demonstrated resilience and how it has shaped the person you are today.

Words of Wisdom: "You are the sky. Everything else—it's just the weather." —Pema Chödrön, *Comfortable with Uncertainty*

From the Bible: "We are hard-pressed in every way, but not crushed; perplexed, but not absolutely with no way out; persecuted, but not abandoned; knocked down, but not destroyed." —2 Corinthians 4:8-9

Reflection Question: How has your resilience helped you navigate life's challenges, and how can you continue to draw strength from this quality?

January 16th: The Power of Vulnerability in Strength

Strength is often seen as the ability to stand firm, but true strength also lies in the willingness to be vulnerable. Vulnerability is not weakness; it's the courage to be open, to admit when you need help, and to face life's uncertainties with grace. For many women, embracing vulnerability is a path to deeper connection and greater inner strength.

Vulnerability is where true strength is born. It allows you to connect with others on a deeper level and to grow beyond your fears. Today, honor the strength it takes to be vulnerable, to show up fully in your life, even when it's uncomfortable.

Words of Wisdom: "In the end, it is not the easy times that define us, but the difficult ones. It is how we embrace uncertainty and risk that makes us stronger." —Wayne Dyer, *There's a Spiritual Solution to Every Problem*

From the Bible: "That is why I take pleasure in weaknesses, in insults, in times of need, in persecutions and difficulties, for when I am weak, then I am powerful." —2 Corinthians 12:10

Reflection Question: How can you embrace vulnerability as a source of strength in your life, allowing it to deepen your connections and your resilience?

January 17th: Harnessing the Energy of Challenges

Every challenge you face carries a unique energy—an opportunity to transform difficulties into personal power. This energy, when harnessed, can propel you forward, helping you to break through barriers and reach new heights. For women, particularly those balancing multiple roles, challenges can feel overwhelming, but they also offer a chance to tap into a deeper well of strength.

Challenges are not obstacles; they are catalysts for growth. By embracing the energy of your challenges, you can turn adversity into a force for positive change in your life. Today, focus on how you can harness this energy to fuel your journey forward.

Words of Wisdom: "When you stay centered and peaceful, the reality of your life will be a reflection of your inner state." —Dr. Joe Dispenza, *Becoming Supernatural*

From the Bible: "Jehovah is my strength and my might; he has become my salvation." —Psalm 118:14

Reflection Question: How can you harness the energy of the challenges you've faced to create positive momentum in your life?

January 18th: Embracing Uncertainty with Strength

Life is full of uncertainties, and it's easy to feel overwhelmed when the path ahead is unclear. But uncertainty is also a space where possibilities are born, where you can grow beyond what you thought was possible. Embracing uncertainty with strength means trusting in the process, even when you don't have all the answers.

Strength comes from embracing the unknown with faith and courage. It's about letting go of the need for control and opening yourself to the possibilities that lie beyond your fears. Today, reflect on how you can approach uncertainty not with dread, but with the confidence that you have the strength to navigate whatever comes your way.

Words of Wisdom: "The only thing that is certain is that everything changes. The secret is to become comfortable with uncertainty." — Pema Chödrön, *Comfortable with Uncertainty*

From the Bible: "Do not be anxious over anything, but in everything by prayer and supplication along with thanksgiving, let your petitions be made known to God." —Philippians 4:6

Reflection Question: How can you embrace the uncertainties in your life with strength, trusting that you have the resilience to handle whatever the future holds?

January 19th: Finding Strength in Community

Strength is often portrayed as an individual quality, but there is immense power in finding strength through community. Whether it's the support of family, friends, or a broader network, being part of a community provides the encouragement, love, and shared wisdom that can help you navigate life's challenges. For many women, especially those juggling multiple roles, community can be a vital source of resilience.

Community is where strength multiplies. By leaning on and supporting others, you find that your own strength is magnified. Today, reflect on the role your community plays in your life and how you can both give and receive strength within it.

Words of Wisdom: "The bond that links your true family is not one of blood but of respect and joy in each other's life." —Richard Bach

From the Bible: "Two are better than one because they have a good reward for their hard work. For if one of them falls, the other can help his partner up." —Ecclesiastes 4:9-10

Reflection Question: How can you draw strength from your community, and in what ways can you contribute to the strength of others?

January 20th: The Strength to Forgive

Forgiveness is one of the most powerful acts of strength a person can exhibit. It's not about condoning the wrongs done to you, but about freeing yourself from the weight of anger and resentment. For many women, carrying the burden of past hurts can hinder personal growth and happiness. Today, focus on the strength it takes to forgive—whether it's forgiving someone else or yourself.

Forgiveness is an act of liberation. It allows you to move forward with peace, releasing the hold that past wounds have on your heart. Reflect on the areas in your life where forgiveness is needed and find the strength to let go.

Words of Wisdom: "Forgiveness is the act of releasing the burden of the past, allowing your heart to heal and bloom anew." —Pema Chodron, *Comfortable with Uncertainty*

From the Bible: "When you stand praying, forgive anyone against whom you have a grievance, so that your Father in the heavens may also forgive you your trespasses." —Mark 11:25

Reflection Question: Where in your life do you need to practice forgiveness, and how can this act of strength bring you peace and healing?

January 21st: Honoring Your Journey

Every step of your journey—every triumph, every setback—has contributed to the strength and resilience you possess today. Honoring your journey means acknowledging the hardships you've overcome, the lessons you've learned, and the person you've become. It's about recognizing that each experience, whether joyous or painful, has played a role in shaping your unique path.

Your journey is a testament to your strength. By honoring it, you celebrate not just the milestones, but the entire process of growth. Today, take time to reflect on your journey and the strength you've demonstrated along the way.

Words of Wisdom: "The only way to make sense out of change is to plunge into it, move with it, and join the dance." —Alan Watts

From the Bible: "I will praise you because in an awe-inspiring way I am wonderfully made. Your works are wonderful, as I well know." —Psalm 139:14

Reflection Question: How can you honor your journey today, acknowledging the strength and resilience that have brought you to where you are now?

Week 4: Nourishing with Self-Compassion

Nourishing your soul with self-compassion is an essential act of kindness towards yourself. In a world where women are often expected to be everything for everyone—caregivers, professionals, friends, and partners—it's easy to forget to care for your own needs with the same gentleness you offer others. This week is dedicated to turning that compassion inward, recognizing that self-care and self-compassion are not luxuries, but necessities.

Self-compassion means embracing yourself with love and understanding, especially in moments of struggle or failure. It's about giving yourself permission to be imperfect, to make mistakes, and to be a work in progress. Rather than being harsh or critical, self-compassion invites you to treat yourself with the same kindness you would offer a dear friend.

January 22nd: Embracing Imperfection

Imperfection is a natural part of being human, yet many of us struggle with accepting our flaws and mistakes. The pursuit of perfection can be exhausting, leading to self-criticism and feelings of inadequacy. Today, focus on embracing your imperfections with compassion. Understand that flaws and mistakes are not signs of failure, but opportunities for growth and learning.

Embrace imperfection as part of your unique journey. Let go of the pressure to be perfect and instead, celebrate the beauty of your imperfections. They make you who you are—a wonderfully complex, evolving individual.

Words of Wisdom: "Imperfection is not our personal problem—it is a natural part of existing." —Pema Chödrön, *Comfortable with Uncertainty*

From the Bible: "For all have sinned and fall short of the glory of God." —Romans 3:23

Reflection Question: How can you be more accepting of your imperfections, and how might this acceptance lead to greater self-compassion?

January 23rd: Speaking Kindly to Yourself

The words you speak to yourself shape your reality. Negative self-talk can be damaging, eroding your self-esteem and making it difficult to see your worth. On the other hand, kind and encouraging words can uplift you, reinforcing your strengths and helping you navigate challenges with grace. Today, focus on speaking kindly to yourself.

Practice self-compassion through your words. Replace negative thoughts with affirmations of your worth and potential. Remind yourself that you are deserving of kindness, especially from yourself.

Words of Wisdom: "Be careful how you are talking to yourself because you are listening." —Lisa M. Hayes

From the Bible: "Death and life are in the power of the tongue, and those who love it will eat its fruit." —Proverbs 18:21

Reflection Question: What negative thoughts do you need to replace with kind and supportive words, and how can this shift impact your self-compassion?

January 24th: Giving Yourself Permission to Rest

In a society that often glorifies busyness, rest can be seen as unproductive or even indulgent. However, rest is a vital part of self-compassion. It allows your body, mind, and spirit to recharge, preventing burnout and maintaining your overall well-being. Today, give yourself permission to rest without guilt.

Rest is not a luxury—it's a necessity. Allow yourself to take a break, whether it's a short nap, a peaceful walk, or simply sitting quietly with your thoughts. By honoring your need for rest, you nourish your soul and prepare yourself to face life's demands with renewed energy.

Words of Wisdom: "You rest deeply only when you let go." — Sadhguru, *Inner Engineering*

From the Bible: "In peace I will both lie down and sleep, for you alone, O Jehovah, make me dwell in security." —Psalm 4:8

Reflection Question: How can you incorporate more rest into your life, and how does giving yourself permission to rest enhance your overall well-being?

January 25th: Celebrating Your Worth

Self-compassion is deeply connected to recognizing and celebrating your worth. You are valuable simply because you exist—not because of your accomplishments, roles, or how well you meet others' expectations. Today, focus on celebrating your inherent worth.

Recognize your value beyond what you do or achieve. Celebrate yourself for who you are at your core—a person deserving of love, respect, and kindness. By honoring your worth, you strengthen your foundation of self-compassion, enabling you to approach life with confidence and inner peace.

Words of Wisdom: "Your task is not to seek for love, but merely to seek and find all the barriers within yourself that you have built against it." —Rumi

From the Bible: "Are not five sparrows sold for two coins of small value? Yet not one of them is forgotten before God. But even the hairs of your head are all numbered. Have no fear; you are worth more than many sparrows." —Luke 12:6-7

Reflection Question: How can you more fully recognize and celebrate your worth, and how does this recognition influence your self-compassion?

January 26th: Letting Go of Self-Judgment

Self-judgment can be one of the harshest forms of criticism we face. It often manifests as an inner voice that is quick to point out mistakes, flaws, and perceived shortcomings. This constant judgment can be exhausting and can hinder your ability to grow and heal. Today, focus on letting go of self-judgment and embracing yourself with kindness and understanding.

Release the weight of self-judgment and embrace acceptance. Understand that being human means making mistakes and that these mistakes do not define your worth. Allow yourself to move forward with compassion and forgiveness, knowing that you are doing the best you can.

Words of Wisdom: "When you are compassionate with yourself, you trust in your soul, which you let guide your life. Your soul knows the geography of your destiny better than you do." —John O'Donohue

From the Bible: "Stop judging, and you will by no means be judged; and stop condemning, and you will by no means be condemned. Keep on forgiving, and you will be forgiven." —Luke 6:37

Reflection Question: What areas of your life have been impacted by self-judgment, and how can releasing this judgment lead to greater self-compassion and peace?

January 27th: Practicing Gratitude for Yourself

Gratitude is often directed outward, toward others or the things we have in life. However, it is equally important to practice gratitude for yourself—your strengths, your resilience, and the progress you've made. Today, focus on expressing gratitude for who you are and the journey you've undertaken.

Acknowledge and appreciate your own contributions to your life. Recognize the effort you've put into growing, healing, and striving to be the best version of yourself. By practicing gratitude for yourself, you reinforce your sense of self-worth and deepen your self-compassion.

Words of Wisdom: "Gratitude is the foundation for a positive mindset and a peaceful heart." —Rhonda Byrne, *The Power*

From the Bible: "I praise you because in an awe-inspiring way I am wonderfully made. Your works are wonderful, as I well know." —Psalm 139:14

Reflection Question: What aspects of yourself are you most grateful for, and how can this gratitude strengthen your relationship with yourself?

January 28th: Setting Boundaries with Love

Setting boundaries is a crucial aspect of self-compassion. It involves knowing your limits and communicating them clearly to others, ensuring that your own needs are met and that you are not overextended. Today, focus on setting and maintaining healthy boundaries in your life.

Boundaries are an act of love for yourself. They protect your time, energy, and emotional well-being, allowing you to thrive rather than just survive. By setting boundaries, you honor your own needs and create space for self-care and self-compassion.

Words of Wisdom: "You teach people how to treat you by deciding what you will and won't accept." **—Wayne Dyer**

From the Bible: "Above all the things that you guard, safeguard your heart, for out of it are the sources of life." —Proverbs 4:23

Reflection Question: What boundaries do you need to set or reinforce in your life, and how can doing so enhance your sense of self-compassion and well-being?

January 29th: Healing Through Self-Forgiveness

Forgiving yourself can be one of the most challenging aspects of self-compassion, especially when you carry guilt or regret over past actions. However, self-forgiveness is essential for healing and moving forward. It allows you to release the past and embrace the present with a renewed sense of peace.

Forgive yourself for the mistakes you've made. Understand that these mistakes are part of your growth, and they do not diminish your worth. By forgiving yourself, you free yourself from the burdens of the past and open the door to healing and self-compassion.

Words of Wisdom: "Forgiveness is the key to inner peace because it is a reflection of loving yourself enough to let go of the pain." —Wayne Dyer, *There's a Spiritual Solution to Every Problem*

From the Bible: "For I will forgive their error, and I will no longer remember their sin." —Jeremiah 31:34

Reflection Question: What past mistakes are you holding onto, and how can self-forgiveness help you heal and move forward with compassion?

January 30th: Embracing the Present Moment

Self-compassion thrives in the present moment. Often, we get caught up in regrets about the past or worries about the future, which can prevent us from being fully present in our lives. Today, focus on embracing the present moment with mindfulness and self-compassion.

The present moment is where life unfolds. By staying grounded in the now, you can fully experience your life as it is, without judgment or anxiety. Embrace each moment with kindness, allowing yourself to simply be, without pressure or expectation.

Words of Wisdom: "Realize deeply that the present moment is all you ever have. Make the NOW the primary focus of your life." —Eckhart Tolle

From the Bible: "So never be anxious about the next day, for the next day will have its own anxieties. Each day has enough of its own troubles." —Matthew 6:34

Reflection Question: How can embracing the present moment enhance your practice of self-compassion and bring more peace into your daily life?

January 31st: Cultivating Ongoing Self-Compassion

As the month comes to a close, it's important to carry forward the lessons of self-compassion you've cultivated. Self-compassion is not a one-time practice, but an ongoing commitment to treating yourself with kindness, understanding, and love. Today, focus on how you can continue to nourish your soul with self-compassion throughout the year.

Make self-compassion a daily practice. Whether through mindfulness, self-care, or simply speaking kindly to yourself, find ways to incorporate self-compassion into your life every day. By doing so, you build a strong foundation for well-being and resilience.

Words of Wisdom: "The love and attention you always thought you wanted from someone else, is the love and attention you first need to give to yourself." —Bryant McGill

From the Bible: "But besides all these things, clothe yourselves with love, for it is a perfect bond of union." —Colossians 3:14

Reflection Question: How can you make self-compassion a regular part of your life, and what practices will you continue to nurture your soul throughout the year?

February: Embracing Self-Love

February is a month often associated with love, but this year, let it be about a deeper, more personal kind of love—the love you cultivate for yourself. Embracing self-love is not about being self-centered; it's about recognizing your own worth and treating yourself with the kindness and compassion you readily offer others. As women, we often find ourselves at the crossroads of many roles—mother, daughter, partner, friend, and professional—each demanding its share of our energy and attention. But how often do we take the time to nurture the most important relationship of all—the one we have with ourselves?

This month is an invitation to reconnect with your own heart. It's a time to celebrate the many forms of love that enrich our lives, from the love we give to others to the love we deserve to give ourselves. As we journey through February, we'll explore what it means to love ourselves fully and unconditionally. This means recognizing our strengths and embracing our imperfections, nurturing the connections that sustain us, and cultivating a deep acceptance of who we are at our core.

Throughout February, you'll be guided to reflect on how love shows up in your life, in all its forms. From celebrating love in your relationships to nurturing connections with loved ones, from embracing self-acceptance to radiating love and compassion to others, this month will be a journey of the heart. By the end of February, my hope is that you will feel more connected to yourself, more compassionate towards your journey, and more inspired to let your love shine brightly in every aspect of your life.

Let February be a month where you prioritize your well-being, honor your heart's desires, and cultivate a love that begins within and radiates outward, touching every corner of your life.

Week 1: Celebrating Love in All Forms

Love is a powerful force that weaves through every aspect of our lives, taking on many shapes and forms. It's the bond you share with family, the connection with friends, the care you show to those in need, and the quiet moments of affection you offer yourself. This week is about celebrating love in all its beautiful and diverse expressions.

Love isn't confined to romantic relationships; it's present in the warmth of a child's hug, the support of a dear friend, the guidance of a mentor, and the compassion we show to strangers. As women, we are often the nurturers, the ones who spread love through our actions, words, and presence. This week, let's focus on recognizing and celebrating the love that surrounds us and flows through us every day.

February 1st: Recognizing the Love in Your Life

Love is all around us, often in the most unexpected places. It's in the smile of a stranger, the warmth of a friend's voice, and the gentle touch of a loved one. Today, take a moment to recognize and appreciate the love that exists in your life. Think about the people who make you feel supported, cherished, and understood. These connections are the threads that weave together the fabric of your life.

Start by expressing gratitude for the love you receive. Whether it's a text from a friend, a hug from your child, or a kind word from a colleague, each act of love is a gift. By acknowledging this love, you open your heart to even more love and deepen your connections with those around you.

Words of Wisdom: "Love is not something you look for. Love is something you become." —Dr. Wayne Dyer, *There's a Spiritual Solution to Every Problem*

From the Bible: "Hatred is what stirs up contentions, but love covers all offenses." —Proverbs 10:12

Reflection Question: How can you more consciously recognize and appreciate the love in your life today?

February 2nd: Expressing Love Through Kindness

Kindness is love in action. It's the small gestures—a smile, a helping hand, a thoughtful note—that show others they are valued and cared for. Today, focus on expressing love through acts of kindness. Whether it's towards a family member, a friend, or even a stranger, these acts of kindness not only brighten someone else's day but also fill your heart with warmth and joy.

Engage in at least one act of kindness today. It could be something as simple as offering a compliment or taking the time to listen to someone who needs to talk. These small acts of love ripple out into the world, creating a more compassionate and connected community.

Words of Wisdom: "Wherever there is a human being, there is an opportunity for kindness." —Seneca

From the Bible: "Put away from yourselves every kind of malicious bitterness, anger, wrath, screaming, and abusive speech, as well as everything injurious." —Ephesians 4:31

Reflection Question: What acts of kindness can you incorporate into your day to express love to those around you?

February 3rd: Celebrating Love in Friendships

Friendship is one of the purest forms of love. It's built on trust, mutual respect, and shared experiences. Friends are the ones who stand by you in times of joy and sorrow, who listen without judgment, and who lift you up when you're feeling down. Today, celebrate the love that exists in your friendships.

Reach out to a friend today to express your appreciation. Whether it's a phone call, a message, or meeting up for coffee, take time to connect and let them know how much they mean to you. Celebrating these bonds strengthens them, creating a lasting foundation of love and support.

Words of Wisdom: "A friend is someone who gives you total freedom to be yourself." —Jim Morrison

From the Bible: "But there is a friend who sticks closer than a brother." —Proverbs 18:24

Reflection Question: How can you celebrate and nurture the love in your friendships today?

February 4th: Practicing Self-Love

Self-love is the foundation of all other forms of love. When you love and accept yourself, you create a space for others to love you as well. However, self-love is often the most challenging form of love to cultivate. Today, focus on practicing self-love by treating yourself with the same kindness and compassion you offer to others.

Take time today to do something that nurtures your soul. Whether it's a relaxing bath, reading a favorite book, or simply taking a moment to breathe and reflect, these acts of self-care are vital to your well-being. Remember, you are worthy of love—especially your own.

Words of Wisdom: "You yourself, as much as anybody in the entire universe, deserve your love and affection." —Buddha

From the Bible: "Do not owe anything to anyone except to love one another; for whoever loves his fellow man has fulfilled the law." — Romans 13:8

Reflection Question: What can you do today to show yourself the love and care that you deserve?

February 5th: Love in Family Bonds

Family is often where we first learn about love—through the care and support of those closest to us. Family bonds, whether with parents, siblings, children, or extended relatives, are some of the most enduring relationships in our lives. Today, take time to celebrate the love that exists within your family. This love may not always be perfect, but it's a powerful force that shapes who we are.

Spend quality time with your family today. This could be sharing a meal, having a heartfelt conversation, or simply enjoying each other's company. These moments of connection reinforce the love that binds your family together, creating lasting memories and deepening your relationships.

Words of Wisdom: "Family is not an important thing. It's everything." —Michael J. Fox

From the Bible: "Honor your father and your mother, so that you may live a long time in the land that Jehovah your God is giving you." — Exodus 20:12

Reflection Question: How can you express and celebrate the love you have for your family today?

February 6th: Love for the Community

Love extends beyond our immediate circle of family and friends. It also includes the broader community we are part of. Community love is about fostering connections, supporting those in need, and contributing to the well-being of others. Today, focus on how you can show love to your community.

Engage in an act of service for your community today. This could be volunteering, supporting a local business, or simply offering a helping hand to a neighbor. When you give back to your community, you help to create a network of support and love that benefits everyone.

Words of Wisdom: "The greatness of a community is most accurately measured by the compassionate actions of its members." —Coretta Scott King

From the Bible: "Let each one keep seeking, not his own advantage, but that of the other person." —1 Corinthians 10:24

Reflection Question: How can you contribute to the love and well-being of your community today?

February 7th: Love for the World

The love we give and receive isn't limited by geography or culture; it's a universal force that connects us all. Love for the world means embracing our shared humanity, showing compassion for others regardless of their background, and caring for the planet we all call home. Today, reflect on how you can extend love to the world around you.

Practice global love by showing kindness to people outside your immediate circle. This could be through acts of kindness towards strangers, supporting global causes, or making environmentally conscious choices. By acting with love on a global scale, you contribute to a world that is more compassionate, connected, and sustainable.

Words of Wisdom: "We are all a part of the same family, the human family." —Lynne McTaggart, *Living the Field*

From the Bible: "For the entire Law has been fulfilled in one commandment: 'You must love your neighbor as yourself.'" —Galatians 5:14

Reflection Question: How can you extend love beyond your immediate environment to make a positive impact on the world?

Week 2: Nurturing Connections with Loved Ones

Relationships are the cornerstone of our lives, providing support, joy, and a sense of belonging. Nurturing these connections is essential, as they require time, attention, and love to flourish. This week, focus on deepening your relationships with those you hold dear—whether they are family, friends, or significant others.

In our busy lives, it's easy to take our loved ones for granted, assuming they'll always be there. However, strong relationships are built on consistent effort and genuine care. This week is an opportunity to pause, reflect, and actively invest in the bonds that matter most to you. By doing so, you strengthen the ties that uplift you and create a foundation of love that can withstand life's challenges.

February 8th: The Power of Listening

One of the most profound ways to nurture your relationships is by truly listening to those you love. In our fast-paced world, it's easy to listen with only half our attention, thinking about what to say next or multitasking while someone is speaking. But deep, attentive listening is an act of love. It shows the other person that they are valued, heard, and understood.

Today, make an effort to listen deeply to your loved ones. Give them your full attention, without interruption or judgment. This act of love not only strengthens your connection but also allows you to understand them on a deeper level. In the quiet space of listening, you create a sanctuary where hearts can speak freely and connections can deepen.

Words of Wisdom: "When you talk, you are only repeating what you already know. But if you listen, you may learn something new." —Dalai Lama

From the Bible: "A mild answer turns away rage, but a harsh word stirs up anger." —Proverbs 15:1

Reflection Question: How can you become a better listener in your relationships, and how might this practice deepen your connection with loved ones?

February 9th: Sharing Meaningful Moments

In the hustle of everyday life, it's easy to overlook the importance of spending quality time with those we love. But it's in these shared moments—whether simple or extraordinary—that our bonds are strengthened. Time spent together, fully present and engaged, is a gift that nurtures your relationships and creates lasting memories.

Today, focus on creating meaningful moments with your loved ones. It could be as simple as a shared meal, a walk together, or a conversation where you both put away distractions. These moments don't have to be grand; what matters is the presence and connection you bring to them.

Words of Wisdom: "The most precious gift we can offer anyone is our attention." —Thich Nhat Hanh

From the Bible: "Let us consider one another so as to incite to love and fine works, not forsaking our meeting together." —Hebrews 10:24-25

Reflection Question: What meaningful moments can you create today to nurture your connection with those you love?

February 10th: Expressing Gratitude

Gratitude is a powerful way to nurture your relationships. When you take the time to express appreciation for the people in your life, you acknowledge their value and the positive impact they have on you. Gratitude not only strengthens your connections but also fosters a deeper sense of love and respect.

Today, express gratitude to someone you love. It could be through a heartfelt note, a phone call, or simply telling them in person what they mean to you. When you show appreciation, you reinforce the bond you share and invite even more love into your relationship.

Words of Wisdom: "Gratitude is not only the greatest of virtues, but the parent of all others." —Cicero

From the Bible: "Persevere in prayer, staying awake in it with thanksgiving." —Colossians 4:2

Reflection Question: How can you make gratitude a regular practice in your relationships, and what impact might this have on the people you love?

February 11th: Forgiveness as an Act of Love

Every relationship has its challenges, and sometimes, these challenges lead to hurt feelings or misunderstandings. Forgiveness is an essential part of nurturing your connections, allowing you to move past the pain and strengthen your bond. Forgiving someone doesn't mean excusing their behavior; it means choosing to let go of resentment and opening your heart to healing.

Today, practice forgiveness in your relationships. Whether it's a small annoyance or a deeper hurt, take a step towards letting go and allowing love to fill the space where anger or disappointment once lived. Forgiveness is an act of love that frees both you and the other person, making room for a deeper, more compassionate connection.

Words of Wisdom: "The moment you forgive, you reclaim your power from the past and step into the freedom of the present." —Michael Singer, *The Untethered Soul*

From the Bible: "Therefore, become imitators of God, as beloved children, and go on walking in love, just as the Christ also loved us and gave himself for us." —Ephesians 5:1-2

Reflection Question: Who in your life needs your forgiveness today, and how can this act of love transform your relationship?

February 12th: Strengthening Bonds Through Vulnerability

Vulnerability is often seen as a weakness, but in reality, it is one of the strongest foundations of love and connection. When you allow yourself to be open and honest with those you care about, you invite deeper intimacy and trust into your relationships. Sharing your fears, dreams, and even your mistakes can strengthen the bonds you share with loved ones.

Today, practice vulnerability in your relationships. Share something from your heart that you might usually keep to yourself. It could be expressing your love more openly, admitting a mistake, or talking about something that's been weighing on you. When you show your true self, you give others the courage to do the same, creating a safe space where love can grow.

Words of Wisdom: "Vulnerability is the birthplace of love, belonging, joy, courage, empathy, and creativity. It is the source of hope, empathy, accountability, and authenticity." —Brené Brown

From the Bible: "Therefore, put away falsehood, each one of you speak truth with his neighbor, because we are members belonging to one another." —Ephesians 4:25

Reflection Question: How can embracing vulnerability in your relationships deepen the love and trust you share with others?

February 13th: Celebrating the Love in Diversity

In every relationship, there are differences—whether in personality, preferences, or perspectives. These differences can sometimes lead to misunderstandings, but they also enrich our connections, bringing new experiences and growth. Celebrating the diversity within your relationships allows you to appreciate the unique qualities that each person brings into your life.

Today, focus on celebrating the diversity in your relationships. Embrace the differences you have with your loved ones, seeing them as opportunities to learn and grow together. By honoring these differences, you foster a more inclusive and understanding environment where love can thrive.

Words of Wisdom: "Unity in diversity is the highest possible attainment of a civilization, a testimony to the most noble possibilities of the human race." —Michael Novak

From the Bible: "There is neither Jew nor Greek, there is neither slave nor freeman, there is neither male nor female, for you are all one in union with Christ Jesus." —Galatians 3:28

Reflection Question: How can you celebrate and embrace the differences in your relationships to strengthen the love and connection you share?

February 14th: Love as a Daily Practice

On Valentine's Day, love is often celebrated in grand gestures, but the most powerful expressions of love are found in the small, everyday actions that show care and appreciation. Love is not just a feeling; it's a daily practice, a choice you make each day to nurture and strengthen your relationships.

Today, focus on making love a daily practice. Whether through a kind word, a thoughtful gesture, or simply being present, let your actions reflect the love you have for the people in your life.

Celebrate love today by being intentional in your actions. Show those you care about that they are valued and appreciated, not just in big moments but in the quiet, everyday ways that truly matter. Remember, love grows and deepens through the small, consistent gestures that convey your commitment and care.

Words of Wisdom: "Love is not something you find. Love is something that finds you." —Loretta Young

From the Bible: "Let all your things take place with love." —1 Corinthians 16:14

Reflection Question: How can you make love a daily practice in your relationships, ensuring that those you care about feel valued and cherished every day?

Week 3: Embracing Self-Acceptance

Self-acceptance is a profound act of self-love. It's about embracing who you are, with all your strengths and imperfections, and finding peace in knowing that you are enough just as you are. This week, we will focus on activities and reflections that help you cultivate self-acceptance, allowing you to embrace yourself fully and without judgment.

February 15th: Acknowledging Your Unique Journey

Every woman's journey is unique, shaped by her experiences, choices, and challenges. Today, take time to acknowledge and honor the path you've walked. Embrace the lessons you've learned and the growth you've experienced along the way.

Write a letter to yourself, reflecting on your life's journey. Highlight the challenges you've overcome, the milestones you've reached, and the person you've become as a result. As you write, allow yourself to feel pride and gratitude for your resilience and courage. This letter is a testament to your strength and the uniqueness of your journey.

Words of Wisdom: "You are allowed to be both a masterpiece and a work in progress, simultaneously." —Sophia Bush

From the Bible: "For you produced my kidneys; you kept me screened off in the belly of my mother. I praise you because in an awe-inspiring way I am wonderfully made. Your works are wonderful, as I well know." —Psalm 139:13-14

Reflection Question: How can acknowledging the uniqueness of your journey help you to embrace and accept yourself more fully?

February 16th: Embracing Your Imperfections

Self-acceptance includes embracing your imperfections, understanding that they are a natural part of being human. Today, focus on letting go of the need to be perfect and instead, celebrate the beauty of your imperfections.

Stand in front of a mirror and take a few moments to really look at yourself. As you do, acknowledge any flaws or imperfections you see, but instead of criticizing them, speak words of kindness and acceptance. Remind yourself that these imperfections are part of what makes you uniquely you. Practice this activity with compassion and without judgment.

Words of Wisdom: "There is a crack in everything, that's how the light gets in." —Leonard Cohen

From the Bible: "Do you not know? Have you not heard? Jehovah is the everlasting God, the Creator of the ends of the earth. He never tires out or grows weary. His understanding is unsearchable." —Isaiah 40:28

Reflection Question: What imperfections can you embrace today, and how can accepting them bring more peace into your life?

February 17th: Letting Go of Comparison

Comparison is the thief of joy and often stands in the way of self-acceptance. Today, focus on letting go of the habit of comparing yourself to others and instead, embrace your own unique qualities and achievements.

Spend some time reflecting on areas of your life where you tend to compare yourself to others. Write down these comparisons and then, one by one, release them. Replace each comparison with an affirmation that celebrates your unique strengths and accomplishments. Keep these affirmations where you can see them as a reminder to honor your own path.

Words of Wisdom: "Comparison is an act of violence against the self."
—Iyanla Vanzant

From the Bible: "But let each one examine his own actions, and then he will have cause for rejoicing in regard to himself alone, and not in comparison with the other person." —Galatians 6:4

Reflection Question: How can letting go of comparison help you focus on your own strengths and journey?

February 18th: Practicing Forgiveness Toward Yourself

Self-acceptance also means forgiving yourself for past mistakes or perceived shortcomings. Holding onto guilt or regret can prevent you from fully accepting and loving yourself. Today, focus on practicing forgiveness toward yourself.

Write down any regrets, mistakes, or burdens you've been carrying. Acknowledge each one, then consciously choose to forgive yourself. You might say out loud, "I forgive myself for [specific mistake], and I release this burden." Afterward, tear up the paper as a symbolic act of letting go and freeing yourself from the weight of the past.

Words of Wisdom: "Forgiveness is giving up the hope that the past could have been any different." —Oprah Winfrey

From the Bible: "If, then, you are bringing your gift to the altar and there you remember that your brother has something against you, leave your gift there in front of the altar, and go away; first make peace with your brother, and then come back and offer your gift." —Matthew 5:23-24

Reflection Question: What can you forgive yourself for today, and how will this act of forgiveness help you embrace self-acceptance?

February 19th: Celebrating Your Strengths

Embracing self-acceptance includes celebrating your strengths and recognizing the gifts you bring to the world. Today, take time to acknowledge and celebrate what makes you strong, capable, and unique.

Make a list of your strengths, talents, and qualities that you're proud of. This can include anything from your resilience, kindness, creativity, to your ability to listen or your sense of humor. Keep this list somewhere visible, and whenever you doubt yourself, revisit it as a reminder of the amazing person you are.

Words of Wisdom: "You have within you right now, everything you need to deal with whatever the world can throw at you." —Brian Tracy

From the Bible: "For God gave us a spirit not of cowardice, but one of power and of love and of soundness of mind." —2 Timothy 1:7

Reflection Question: How can celebrating your strengths help you build a deeper sense of self-acceptance?

February 20th: Surrounding Yourself with Positive Affirmations

The words you speak to yourself have great power in shaping your self-perception. Today, focus on surrounding yourself with positive affirmations that reinforce self-acceptance and love.

Create a list of positive affirmations that resonate with you, such as "I am enough," "I love and accept myself as I am," or "I am worthy of love and respect." Write these affirmations on sticky notes and place them around your home—on your mirror, in your car, or at your workspace. Repeat these affirmations throughout the day, especially when self-doubt creeps in.

Words of Wisdom: "What lies behind us and what lies before us are tiny matters compared to what lies within us." —Ralph Waldo Emerson

From the Bible: "Speaking thoughtlessly is like the stabs of a sword, but the tongue of the wise is a healing." —Proverbs 12:18

Reflection Question: How can incorporating positive affirmations into your daily routine reinforce your journey toward self-acceptance?

February 21st: Embracing Love—For Yourself

On this day, often associated with expressing love to others, take a moment to turn that love inward. Embrace the love you have for yourself, knowing that self-love is the foundation of all other relationships in your life.

Treat yourself to something special today—a favorite meal, a long bath, a walk in nature, or simply time alone to reflect and relax. As you do, focus on appreciating the person you are. Write a love letter to yourself, acknowledging all the ways you are proud of who you are and how far you've come. Let this letter be a reminder of your commitment to self-love and acceptance.

Words of Wisdom: "You yourself, as much as anybody in the entire universe, deserve your love and affection." —Buddha

From the Bible: "Let all your things take place with love." —1 Corinthians 16:14

Reflection Question: How can embracing love for yourself enhance your overall sense of well-being and happiness?

Week 4: Radiating Love and Compassion

As we enter the final week of February, our focus shifts to radiating love and compassion outward into the world. The love and compassion you cultivate within yourself are powerful forces that can influence the lives of others in profound ways. This week is about taking that inner warmth and extending it to those around you, creating ripples of kindness and understanding that touch every part of your life.

Radiating love and compassion means going beyond your immediate circle of family and friends. It's about embracing a broader, more inclusive perspective that sees the humanity in every person you encounter. It's about showing kindness to strangers, offering support to those in need, and approaching every situation with a heart full of empathy. By doing so, you not only enhance the well-being of others but also deepen your own sense of connection and fulfillment.

February 22nd: Practicing Mindfulness to Radiate Peace

Mindfulness is the art of being fully present in the moment, and it's a powerful way to cultivate inner peace. When you practice mindfulness, you become more aware of your thoughts, emotions, and surroundings, allowing you to respond to life with calm and clarity. This sense of inner peace naturally radiates outward, influencing your interactions with others and creating a more harmonious environment.

Today, dedicate time to mindfulness meditation. Find a quiet space where you can sit comfortably and focus on your breath. As thoughts arise, simply acknowledge them and let them pass without judgment. This practice will help you center yourself, fostering a peace that you can carry with you throughout the day, spreading calmness to those around you.

Words of Wisdom: "Peace comes from within. Do not seek it without."
—Buddha

From the Bible: "But the wisdom from above is first of all pure, then peaceable, reasonable, ready to obey, full of mercy and good fruits, impartial, not hypocritical." —James 3:17

Reflection Question: How can you incorporate mindfulness into your daily routine to cultivate inner peace and radiate it to those around you?

February 23rd: Spreading Peace Through Acts of Kindness

Kindness is a tangible way to radiate love and compassion in the world. Simple acts of kindness—whether it's offering a compliment, helping someone in need, or just being there for a friend—can have a profound impact on the recipient and can create a ripple effect of positivity. When you choose to act kindly, you spread peace and harmony, making the world a better place, one small act at a time.

Today, engage in a deliberate act of kindness. Whether it's something small like holding the door open for someone or something more involved like volunteering your time, each act of kindness helps to build a more compassionate community. Remember, no act is too small; each one contributes to the collective peace we all desire.

Words of Wisdom: "Hatred does not cease by hatred, but only by love; this is the eternal rule." —Buddha

From the Bible: "Happy are the peacemakers, since they will be called sons of God." —Matthew 5:9

Reflection Question: What act of kindness can you perform today to spread peace and compassion to those around you?

February 24th: Creating Peace in Relationships

Peaceful relationships are built on mutual respect, understanding, and effective communication. When conflicts arise, it's essential to approach them with a calm and understanding demeanor, seeking resolution through dialogue and compromise. By fostering peaceful interactions, you not only strengthen your relationships but also contribute to a more peaceful environment overall.

Today, focus on resolving any conflicts in your relationships peacefully. Approach any disagreements with a spirit of understanding and a willingness to listen. Seek common ground and work towards solutions that honor both your needs and the needs of others. This approach will help maintain harmony and reinforce the bonds you share.

Words of Wisdom: "The fruit of righteousness is sown in peaceful conditions for those who are making peace." —James 3:18

From the Bible: "If possible, as far as it depends on you, be peaceable with all men." —Romans 12:18

Reflection Question: How can you foster peaceful resolutions in your relationships, and what steps can you take today to maintain harmony with those around you?

February 25th: Volunteering to Spread Love and Compassion

Volunteering is a powerful way to extend your love and compassion beyond your immediate circle and into the broader community. By giving your time and energy to help others, you contribute to the well-being of your community and radiate love in a tangible way. Volunteering not only benefits those you serve but also enriches your own life, deepening your sense of purpose and connection.

Today, find an opportunity to volunteer in your community. Whether it's helping at a local shelter, participating in a clean-up effort, or supporting a cause you care about, your contributions can make a significant difference. Through volunteering, you embody the love and compassion you wish to see in the world.

Words of Wisdom: "Lord, make me an instrument of your peace. Where there is hatred, let me sow love." —St. Francis of Assisi

From the Bible: "Moreover, do not forget to do good and to share what you have with others, for God is well-pleased with such sacrifices." —Hebrews 13:16

Reflection Question: How can you use your time and talents to volunteer and spread love and compassion in your community?

February 26th: Embracing Forgiveness as a Path to Peace

Forgiveness is one of the most profound ways to cultivate inner peace and radiate it outward. Holding onto anger or resentment can disrupt your peace and strain your relationships. However, when you choose to forgive, you release the burden of negativity and open your heart to healing and reconciliation. Forgiveness doesn't mean forgetting or excusing hurtful actions, but rather, it's a decision to let go and move forward in peace.

Today, focus on forgiving someone who has wronged you, or forgive yourself for past mistakes. Allow forgiveness to bring peace to your heart and relationships, creating space for love and understanding to grow.

Words of Wisdom: "Holding on to anger is like grasping a hot coal with the intent of throwing it at someone else; you are the one who gets burned." —Buddha

From the Bible: "Keep on forgiving, and you will be forgiven." —Luke 6:37

Reflection Question: How can embracing forgiveness help you restore peace within yourself and your relationships?

February 27th: Cultivating Peace Through Active Listening

Active listening is a powerful tool for fostering peace in your interactions with others. When you listen attentively and without judgment, you create a safe space for open and honest communication. This practice not only strengthens your relationships but also helps to resolve conflicts and misunderstandings before they escalate.

Today, practice active listening in your conversations. Focus on truly hearing what the other person is saying, without interrupting or planning your response while they speak. This mindful approach can transform your interactions, making them more peaceful and constructive.

Words of Wisdom: "True listening is a silent form of love, allowing others the space to be heard and understood." —Michael Singer, *The Untethered Soul*

From the Bible: "The one guarding his mouth and his tongue keeps himself out of trouble." —Proverbs 21:23

Reflection Question: How can practicing active listening improve the peace and understanding in your relationships?

February 28th: Spreading Peace Through Gratitude

Gratitude is a simple yet powerful practice that can transform your outlook on life and improve your relationships. When you focus on the positive aspects of your life and express appreciation for the people around you, you create an environment of peace and contentment. Gratitude shifts your perspective from what's lacking to what's abundant, allowing you to radiate positivity and peace.

Today, practice expressing gratitude in all your interactions. Thank someone for their kindness, acknowledge the good in your life, and let gratitude be the lens through which you see the world. This practice will not only bring you peace but also spread it to those around you.

Words of Wisdom: "Gratitude makes sense of our past, brings peace for today, and creates a vision for tomorrow." —Melody Beattie

From the Bible: "Whatever you do, work at it whole-souled as for Jehovah and not for men." —Colossians 3:17

Reflection Question: How can you cultivate a daily practice of gratitude to enhance your inner peace and positively impact those around you?

February 29th: Finding Peace in Nature

Nature has a remarkable ability to restore our sense of peace and balance. The natural world, with its rhythms and cycles, reminds us of the larger picture and helps us reconnect with the present moment. Spending time in nature can quiet the mind, soothe the spirit, and help you find the inner peace that often eludes you in the busyness of everyday life.

Today, take a walk in nature or spend time outdoors. Whether it's a local park, a garden, or a quiet spot where you can observe the beauty around you, allow nature to calm your mind and bring peace to your heart. Let the sights, sounds, and smells of the natural world remind you of the simplicity and serenity that is always available to you.

Words of Wisdom: "Look deep into nature, and then you will understand everything better." —Albert Einstein

From the Bible: "For his invisible qualities are clearly seen from the world's creation onward, because they are perceived by the things made, even his eternal power and Godship, so that they are inexcusable." —Romans 1:20

Reflection Question: How can spending time in nature help you cultivate a deeper sense of peace and connection to the world around you?

Chapter 2: Spring
Renewal and Rebirth

Spring is a season of renewal and rebirth, a time when the world awakens from the stillness of winter and bursts forth with new life. Just as nature begins to blossom, so too can we embrace this season as an opportunity for personal growth and transformation. Spring invites us to shed the old, nurture the seeds of our intentions, and step into a season of joy and vitality.

March is a time of embracing new beginnings. The theme of this month is about awakening to self-love, cultivating gratitude for growth, and nurturing the seeds of intention you've planted. This period is not just about external changes but also about the inner work that allows you to blossom into your fullest self.

April continues this journey of growth by focusing on cultivating inner strength. This month, you'll be guided to clear away emotional clutter, plant seeds of forgiveness, and embrace vulnerability as a pathway to resilience. Spring's energy of renewal is a reminder that true strength comes from being open and compassionate with yourself. As you bloom with resilience, you'll discover the joy that comes from facing challenges with grace and courage.

May brings a deeper connection with nature and self. Grounding in the present moment, flowing with life's changes, and reflecting on your growth are the focus of this month. This is a time to celebrate both inner and outer beauty, recognizing the transformation that has taken place within you. The fruitage of the spirit—joy—will flourish as you embrace the harmony between your inner world and the natural world around you, leading to a season of renewal and rebirth in every aspect of your life.

March: Embracing New Beginnings

March ushers in the first signs of spring, a season synonymous with renewal and rebirth. This is a time when nature awakens from its winter slumber, and the world around us begins to bloom with new life. The changes we observe in nature mirror the transformations we can invite into our own lives. March is an opportunity to embrace new beginnings, to let go of the old, and to welcome fresh possibilities with open arms.

This month, we focus on awakening to self-love, cultivating gratitude for our growth, nurturing the seeds of intention we've planted, and ultimately blossoming into self-compassion. Each week will guide you through these themes, encouraging you to reflect on your personal journey and to take deliberate steps towards the life you desire. Just as the earth begins to thaw and the days grow longer, allow your heart and mind to open up to the potential that lies within you.

March is also a reminder of the importance of patience. As nature shows us, growth and transformation take time. The seeds we plant now—whether they are intentions, habits, or relationships—will require nurturing and care. Trust in the process, knowing that each small step you take is bringing you closer to the person you want to become.

Let March be a time of gentle reflection and purposeful action. Celebrate the new beginnings in your life, no matter how small, and approach each day with a sense of wonder and gratitude. As you move through this month, may you find joy in the journey and strength in the knowledge that you are continuously growing and evolving. The renewal that spring brings is not just in the world around you, but within you as well. Embrace it fully, and let the spirit of spring guide you towards a season of rebirth and renewal.

Week 1: Awakening to Self-Love

Self-love is the foundation upon which all other forms of love are built. It's not about vanity or selfishness, but about recognizing your inherent worth and treating yourself with the kindness and compassion you deserve. Awakening to self-love means embracing who you are, both your strengths and your flaws, and understanding that you are worthy of love and respect simply because you exist.

This week is an invitation to reconnect with yourself, to explore what it means to truly love and care for your own well-being. In the busyness of life, it's easy to forget about your own needs as you focus on caring for others. But self-love is essential; it's the source from which you draw the strength to love others fully and to navigate life's challenges with resilience and grace.

March 1st: Embracing Your Uniqueness

Every woman is a unique tapestry of experiences, strengths, and dreams. Yet, in a world that often pressures us to conform, it can be challenging to fully embrace our individuality. Today is about celebrating the qualities that make you who you are—those quirks, passions, and traits that set you apart from everyone else. When you embrace your uniqueness, you honor the person you were created to be.

Take a moment today to reflect on what makes you unique. Consider the qualities that you admire in yourself, and give yourself permission to stand confidently in your own light. Remember, there is no one else in the world exactly like you, and that is your superpower.

Words of Wisdom: "You are not a drop in the ocean. You are the entire ocean in a drop." —Rumi

From the Bible: "I will praise you because I am fearfully and wonderfully made; your works are wonderful, I know that full well." —Psalm 139:14

Reflection Question: How can you embrace and celebrate your uniqueness today, allowing it to shine brightly in all that you do?

March 2nd: Practicing Self-Compassion

Many of us are our own harshest critics, often holding ourselves to impossible standards. But self-love begins with self-compassion—the practice of being kind and understanding toward yourself, especially when you stumble or make mistakes. Today, let go of the need for perfection and give yourself the grace to be human.

Today, practice self-compassion by speaking kindly to yourself. When you notice negative self-talk creeping in, pause and replace those thoughts with words of encouragement and understanding. Treat yourself with the same kindness you would offer a dear friend.

Words of Wisdom: "You, yourself, as much as anybody in the entire universe, deserve your love and affection." —Buddha

From the Bible: "Jehovah is merciful and compassionate, slow to anger and abundant in loyal love." —Psalm 103:8

Reflection Question: What can you do today to cultivate self-compassion, especially in moments when you feel inadequate or frustrated?

March 3rd: Nurturing Your Inner Joy

True joy is not dependent on external circumstances; it is an inner state that can be nurtured through a deep connection with yourself. Joy comes from living authentically and finding contentment in the simple moments of life. Today is about nurturing that inner joy by connecting with what truly makes your heart sing.

Take time today to do something that brings you joy. Whether it's a hobby, spending time in nature, or simply savoring a quiet moment with a cup of tea, let yourself bask in the simple pleasures that life offers. Joy is a gift you give to yourself.

Words of Wisdom: "Joy is what happens to us when we allow ourselves to recognize how good things really are." —Marianne Williamson

—

From the Bible: "The joy of Jehovah is your strength." —Nehemiah 8:10

Reflection Question: What small action can you take today to nurture the joy that lives within you, regardless of your external circumstances?

March 4th: Honoring Your Boundaries

Self-love includes setting and honoring boundaries that protect your energy and well-being. It's about recognizing your limits and not being afraid to say "no" when something doesn't serve you. Boundaries are an essential part of maintaining a healthy relationship with yourself and others.

Today, reflect on where you need to set or reinforce boundaries in your life. Whether it's in your personal or professional relationships, honor your needs by clearly communicating your limits. Remember, setting boundaries is an act of love, both for yourself and for those around you.

Words of Wisdom: "You teach people how to treat you by what you allow, what you stop, and what you reinforce." —Tony Gaskins

From the Bible: "Just let your word 'Yes' mean Yes, and your 'No,' No." —Matthew 5:37

Reflection Question: Where in your life do you need to set or strengthen boundaries to protect your well-being, and how can you take a step toward doing that today?

March 5th: Prioritizing Self-Care

Self-care is more than just pampering yourself; it's about making your well-being a priority. It's recognizing that taking care of your physical, emotional, and mental health is essential to living a balanced and fulfilling life. Today, focus on how you can incorporate self-care into your routine, treating it as a non-negotiable part of your day.

Choose one self-care activity that truly nourishes you. This could be anything from taking a relaxing bath, going for a walk-in nature, practicing yoga, or reading a good book. Schedule this time as you would any other important appointment, and honor it without guilt or distraction. Let this be a time just for you, to recharge and connect with yourself.

Words of Wisdom: "Self-care is how you take your power back." — Lalah Delia

From the Bible: "So let us not give up in doing what is fine, for in due season we will reap if we do not tire out." —Galatians 6:9

Reflection Question: What self-care practices can you commit to regularly, ensuring that your well-being remains a priority in your life?

March 6th: Cultivating Positive Self-Talk

The way you talk to yourself shapes your self-perception and influences how you navigate the world. Positive self-talk is a powerful tool for nurturing self-love, helping you build confidence and resilience. Today, focus on cultivating a habit of speaking kindly to yourself, especially in moments of doubt or difficulty.

Throughout the day, consciously replace negative thoughts with positive affirmations. For example, if you catch yourself thinking, "I can't do this," replace it with, "I am capable, and I can figure this out." Write down a few affirmations that resonate with you and repeat them whenever you need a boost of confidence. Let your words lift you up rather than hold you back.

Words of Wisdom: "What you tell yourself every day will either lift you up or tear you down." —**Michael Singer**

From the Bible: "The words of a man's mouth are deep waters. The fountain of wisdom is a bubbling brook." —Proverbs 18:4

Reflection Question: How can you change your inner dialogue to be more supportive and inspiring, and what positive affirmations will you carry with you today?

March 7th: Embracing Your Body with Love

Self-love includes embracing your body—acknowledging its strength, beauty, and the life it supports. In a world that often promotes unrealistic standards, it's important to practice body positivity and treat your body with the respect and love it deserves. Today, focus on honoring your body as it is, appreciating all it does for you.

Spend a few moments in front of a mirror, and instead of focusing on perceived flaws, express gratitude for your body. Consider the ways it serves you daily, from carrying you through life's tasks to allowing you to experience the world. Engage in a loving activity for your body, whether it's a gentle stretch, a nourishing meal, or simply resting when you need to. Let today be about embracing and celebrating your body in its entirety.

Words of Wisdom: "Your body is precious. It is your vehicle for awakening. Treat it with care." —**Buddha**

From the Bible: "I will praise you because in an awe-inspiring way I am wonderfully made. Your works are wonderful, as I well know." —Psalm 139:14

Reflection Question: How can you practice gratitude for your body today, and what actions can you take to show it the love and care it deserves?

Week 2: Cultivating Gratitude for Growth

Gratitude is a powerful force that can transform the way we see ourselves and our lives. It's easy to focus on what we lack or the challenges we face, but this week invites you to shift your perspective. By cultivating gratitude, especially for the growth you've experienced, you open your heart to even more blessings and personal development.

Growth isn't always easy. It often comes through challenges, setbacks, and moments of discomfort. But these are the very experiences that shape us into who we are meant to become. This week is about recognizing the value of these experiences, no matter how difficult they may have been, and expressing gratitude for the lessons they've taught you.

Each day this week, you'll be encouraged to reflect on the ways you've grown, both in the past and in the present. You'll explore how gratitude can turn even the hardest times into opportunities for learning and how acknowledging your progress can fuel further growth. As you practice gratitude, you'll find that it not only enhances your well-being but also deepens your appreciation for the journey of life.

March 8th: Gratitude for Challenges

It's easy to be grateful for the good things in life, but true growth often comes from the challenges we face. The obstacles we encounter, though difficult, are opportunities for learning and personal development. Today, instead of focusing on the difficulty of a challenge, try to see it as a stepping stone towards becoming the person you are meant to be.

Reflect on a recent challenge you've faced and find something to be grateful for in that experience. Whether it's a lesson learned, a new strength discovered, or a deeper understanding gained, acknowledge the growth that has come from this challenge. Gratitude for these moments helps you to embrace the fullness of your life's journey.

Words of Wisdom: "What you focus on expands. Keep your mind on your purpose, and the obstacles will diminish." —Rhonda Byrne, *The Power*

From the Bible: "Rejoice in the hope. Endure under tribulation. Persevere in prayer." —Romans 12:12

Reflection Question: How can you shift your perspective to see challenges as opportunities for growth, and what can you be grateful for in a current or past challenge?

March 9th: Gratitude for Relationships

Relationships are one of life's greatest blessings. They provide us with support, love, and companionship, and they also challenge us to grow in ways we never imagined. Whether it's with family, friends, or a partner, your relationships have shaped you and helped you become who you are today.

Today, express gratitude for the relationships in your life that have contributed to your growth. Reach out to someone who has had a positive impact on you and let them know how much you appreciate them. A simple "thank you" can go a long way in deepening your connection and nurturing your relationships.

Words of Wisdom: "Gratitude turns what we have into enough, and more." —Melody Beattie

From the Bible: "Earnestly endeavor to maintain the oneness of the spirit in the uniting bond of peace." —Ephesians 4:3

Reflection Question: How have your relationships helped you grow, and how can you show gratitude for the people who have supported you along the way?

March 10th: Gratitude for Inner Strength

There are times in life when we are called to dig deep and find the strength, we didn't know we had. This inner strength often reveals itself in moments of adversity, when we are pushed to our limits and forced to rely on our faith, resilience, and determination. Today, take a moment to acknowledge and be grateful for the inner strength that has carried you through tough times.

Spend time today reflecting on a moment when you had to rely on your inner strength. How did this experience shape you, and what did you learn about yourself? Express gratitude for the resilience and courage that helped you navigate that situation.

Words of Wisdom: "Strength does not come from physical capacity. It comes from an indomitable will." —Mahatma Gandhi

From the Bible: "For you know that the quality of your faith produces endurance. But let endurance complete its work, so that you may be complete and sound in all respects, not lacking in anything." —James 1:3-4

Reflection Question: How has your inner strength supported your growth, and how can you continue to cultivate this strength moving forward?

March 11th: Gratitude for Growth Through Patience

Growth often requires patience, especially when we are eager to see results or reach our goals. Patience teaches us to trust the process, to understand that progress takes time, and to appreciate the journey rather than rushing to the destination. Today, focus on the growth that has come from your practice of patience.

Today, identify an area of your life where patience has led to significant growth. Reflect on how waiting, enduring, and staying committed to the process has shaped you and brought you closer to your goals. Express gratitude for the patience that has allowed you to grow in wisdom and understanding.

Words of Wisdom: "Patience is not the ability to wait, but the ability to keep a good attitude while waiting." —Joyce Meyer

From the Bible: "Look! The farmer keeps waiting for the precious fruit of the earth, exercising patience over it until it gets the early rain and the late rain." —James 5:7

Reflection Question: How has practicing patience contributed to your growth, and how can you continue to embrace patience as a vital part of your personal development?

March 12th: Gratitude for Spiritual Growth

Spiritual growth is an essential aspect of personal development. It's the process through which we deepen our understanding of life's mysteries, cultivate a sense of peace, and connect with something greater than ourselves. This growth often happens quietly, over time, as we navigate life's experiences and challenges. Today, focus on the ways your spiritual journey has shaped you.

Take time today to reflect on your spiritual growth and express gratitude for the insights and wisdom you've gained. Whether it's through meditation, prayer, or contemplation, acknowledge the role that your spiritual practices have played in your personal evolution.

Words of Wisdom: "The purpose of life is spiritual growth." —Leo Tolstoy

From the Bible: "On the other hand, the fruitage of the spirit is love, joy, peace, patience, kindness, goodness, faith." —Galatians 5:22

Reflection Question: How has your spiritual growth influenced your life, and what practices can you continue to nurture this aspect of your journey?

March 13th: Gratitude for Life's Simple Pleasures

In our pursuit of big goals and dreams, we sometimes overlook the simple pleasures that bring joy to our everyday lives. These small moments—like the warmth of the sun on your skin, the taste of your favorite meal, or the sound of laughter—are gifts that enrich our lives in ways we often take for granted. Today, cultivate gratitude for these simple joys.

Today, pay attention to the small pleasures that bring you joy. Whether it's enjoying a cup of coffee in the morning, taking a walk in nature, or spending time with loved ones, savor these moments and express gratitude for the happiness they bring.

Words of Wisdom: "Enjoy the little things in life, for one day you may look back and realize they were the big things." —Robert Brault

From the Bible: "Better is the end of a matter than its beginning. Better to be patient than to be haughty in spirit." —Ecclesiastes 7:8

Reflection Question: What simple pleasures in your life bring you the most joy, and how can you cultivate more gratitude for these moments?

March 14th: Gratitude for Personal Growth

Personal growth is a journey that is often marked by both triumphs and challenges. It's the process of becoming more of who you truly are, learning from your experiences, and evolving into the best version of yourself. Today, celebrate the progress you've made on your personal growth journey, no matter how big or small.

Take some time today to reflect on the personal growth you've experienced over the past year. Acknowledge the lessons you've learned, the strengths you've developed, and the person you are becoming. Express gratitude for the journey and the progress you've made.

Words of Wisdom: "The only person you are destined to become is the person you decide to be." —Ralph Waldo Emerson

---

From the Bible: "Keep this mental attitude in you that was also in Christ Jesus." —Philippians 2:5

Reflection Question: How have you grown personally over the past year, and what steps can you take to continue this journey of growth and self-discovery?

Week 3: Nurturing Seeds of Intention

Intentions are the seeds we plant in the garden of our lives, and like any garden, they require care and attention to grow. This week is dedicated to nurturing the intentions you've set for yourself—those goals, dreams, and desires that reflect your deepest aspirations. Whether these intentions are related to your personal growth, relationships, or life's purpose, they need to be tended to with patience, focus, and a gentle heart.

Nurturing your intentions involves more than just setting goals; it's about aligning your thoughts, emotions, and actions with what you truly want to achieve. It's about being mindful of the choices you make each day, ensuring that they contribute to the growth of your intentions. Just as a gardener waters, prunes, and protects their plants, you too must nurture your intentions with consistency and care.

March 15th: Setting Clear Intentions

The first step in nurturing your intentions is to make them clear and specific. Vague intentions are like seeds scattered in the wind—they may land anywhere, and not all will take root. When you set clear intentions, you provide direction for your energy and focus, making it easier to manifest what you truly desire.

Today, take time to clearly define your intentions. Write them down and be specific about what you want to achieve. Visualize these intentions as seeds you are planting in your life, and imagine the growth that will come as you nurture them.

Words of Wisdom: "The clearer you are about what you want, the more power you will have to achieve it." —Billy Cox

From the Bible: "Keep on asking, and it will be given you; keep on seeking, and you will find; keep on knocking, and it will be opened to you." —Matthew 7:7

Reflection Question: What are the specific intentions you want to nurture in your life, and how can you clearly define them to guide your actions?

March 16th: Aligning Actions with Intentions

Intentions are powerful, but they require action to bring them to life. It's not enough to simply set an intention; you must also take consistent steps toward achieving it. These actions, no matter how small, are the nurturing process that allows your intentions to grow and flourish.

Today, focus on aligning your actions with your intentions. Choose one intention you've set and identify the actions you can take today to support it. Remember, even small steps are progress. Celebrate each action as a nurturing force for your intentions.

Words of Wisdom: "Intentions are the driving force behind our actions. When aligned, they propel us toward our goals with grace and power." —Rhonda Byrne

From the Bible: "Let us not give up in doing what is fine, for in due season we will reap if we do not tire out." —Galatians 6:9

Reflection Question: What actions can you take today that align with your intentions, and how can you make these actions a consistent part of your daily routine?

March 17th: Overcoming Obstacles

Every journey of growth will encounter obstacles—moments when it feels as though your intentions are being tested. These challenges are a

---

natural part of the process and often provide valuable lessons that strengthen your resolve. The key is to view obstacles not as setbacks, but as opportunities to reassess, adapt, and continue moving forward.

Today, identify any obstacles that are hindering the growth of your intentions. Reflect on how you can overcome these challenges with patience and perseverance. Consider what adjustments you might need to make to keep your intentions on track.

Words of Wisdom: "Obstacles are those frightful things you see when you take your eyes off your goal." —Henry Ford

From the Bible: "For all things I have the strength through the one who gives me power." —Philippians 4:13

Reflection Question: What obstacles are you facing in nurturing your intentions, and how can you approach these challenges with resilience and creativity?

March 18th: Trusting the Process

Nurturing intentions requires patience and trust in the process. Just as a seed takes time to grow into a plant, your intentions need time to manifest. It's easy to become impatient when results aren't immediate, but remember that growth often happens beneath the surface before it becomes visible. Trust that your efforts are laying the foundation for something beautiful.

Today, practice trusting in the timing of your intentions. Reflect on the progress you've made so far, even if it seems small. Remind yourself that every step forward is a step closer to your goals, and that sometimes, the most important growth happens when you're not looking.

Words of Wisdom: "Patience is not simply the ability to wait—it's how we behave while we're waiting." —Joyce Meyer

From the Bible: "Be patient, then, brothers, until the presence of the Lord. Look! The farmer keeps waiting for the precious fruit of the earth,

exercising patience over it until it gets the early rain and the late rain." —
James 5:7

Reflection Question: How can you cultivate patience and trust in the process of nurturing your intentions, even when results are not immediately visible?

March 19th: Watering Your Intentions with Positivity

Just as plants need water to grow, your intentions need to be nurtured with positivity and hope. The energy you bring to your intentions influences how they manifest in your life. By maintaining a positive outlook and speaking words of encouragement over your goals, you help create an environment where your intentions can thrive.

Today, focus on watering your intentions with positive thoughts and affirmations. Speak life into your goals, reminding yourself that you are capable of achieving what you've set out to do. Surround your intentions with positivity and watch them grow.

Words of Wisdom: "What you think, you become. What you feel, you attract. What you imagine, you create." —Buddha

From the Bible: "Pleasant sayings are a honeycomb, sweet to the soul and a healing to the bones." —Proverbs 16:24

Reflection Question: What positive affirmations can you speak over your intentions today to encourage their growth and success?

March 20th: Cultivating Patience with Yourself

Growth is a process, and sometimes it can feel like you're not making progress fast enough. But just as it takes time for seeds to grow into strong plants, it takes time for your intentions to manifest fully in your life. Cultivating patience with yourself is essential during this process. Be gentle and compassionate with yourself as you nurture your intentions.

Today, practice self-compassion by acknowledging your progress, no matter how small. Reflect on the growth you've experienced, and remind yourself that each step forward is significant. Give yourself the grace to grow at your own pace.

Words of Wisdom: "Patience means allowing things to unfold at their own pace rather than trying to force them" —Pema Chodron

From the Bible: "Happy is the man who keeps on enduring trial, because on becoming approved he will receive the crown of life, which Jehovah promised to those who continue loving him." —James 1:12

Reflection Question: How can you show patience and compassion to yourself during your growth process, and what progress can you celebrate today?

March 21st: Celebrating Small Wins

In the journey of nurturing your intentions, it's important to celebrate the small wins along the way. These small successes are the milestones that mark your progress and remind you that you're on the right path. Celebrating these moments not only boosts your confidence but also fuels your motivation to keep moving forward.

Today, take time to celebrate a small win in your journey. Reflect on the steps you've taken and acknowledge the progress you've made. Whether it's a completed task, a positive change in mindset, or a moment of clarity, honor these achievements as vital parts of your growth.

Words of Wisdom: "Success is the sum of small efforts, repeated day in and day out." —Robert Collier

From the Bible: "Always rejoice. Pray constantly. Give thanks for everything; for this is God's will for you in Christ Jesus." —1 Thessalonians 5:16-18

Reflection Question: What small win can you celebrate today, and how does acknowledging this achievement motivate you to continue nurturing your intentions?

Week 4: Blossoming into Self-Compassion

Self-compassion is the gentle understanding that you are human, capable of both great strength and vulnerability. It's about treating yourself with the same kindness, care, and forgiveness that you so freely offer to others. As women, we often carry the weight of the world on our shoulders, striving to meet every expectation, often at the cost of our own well-being. This week, let's focus on blossoming into self-compassion, embracing the beauty of being perfectly imperfect.

Just as a flower blooms in its own time, so too should we allow ourselves to grow and flourish without the harsh judgment or unrealistic expectations we often place upon ourselves. Each day this week, we'll explore ways to practice self-compassion through patience, kindness, and understanding. By nurturing this essential quality within ourselves, we can create a more loving and supportive inner environment, which will naturally extend to those around us.

March 22nd: Embrace the Transition

March is a time of change and renewal, both in nature and in our lives. Just as the earth transitions from winter to spring, we too experience periods of growth that require patience and understanding. Embrace these transitions with compassion, allowing yourself the grace to move through changes at your own pace.

Today, be patient with yourself as you navigate any changes or challenges in your life. Recognize that growth takes time, and it's okay if everything doesn't fall into place immediately. Allow yourself to experience this transition without pressure or self-criticism.

Words of Wisdom: "The only way to make sense out of change is to plunge into it, move with it, and join the dance." —Alan Watts

From the Bible: "The one who is slow to anger has great discernment, but the impatient one displays his foolishness." —Proverbs 14:29

Reflection Question: How can you show patience and compassion to yourself as you move through transitions and changes in your life?

March 23rd: Practice Mindfulness and Self-Care

Mindfulness and self-care are essential practices in cultivating self-compassion. By taking the time to slow down and tune into your own needs, you create a space where you can be kind and gentle with yourself. These practices help ground you in the present moment, allowing you to approach life with greater patience and peace.

Today, dedicate time to mindfulness and self-care. Whether it's through meditation, journaling, or simply taking a walk in nature, use this time to connect with yourself and practice being fully present. Let this be a moment of calm and kindness towards yourself.

Words of Wisdom: "Self-care is not selfish; you cannot serve from an empty vessel." —Eleanor Brownn

From the Bible: "Let your love be without hypocrisy. Abhor what is wicked; cling to what is good." —Romans 12:9

Reflection Question: What self-care practice can you incorporate into your day to help nurture your sense of self-compassion and inner peace?

March 24th: Set Realistic Expectations

It's easy to fall into the trap of expecting too much from ourselves—trying to do it all, be it all, without acknowledging our own limits. Setting realistic expectations is a form of self-compassion that allows you to honor where you are in your journey. It's about giving yourself permission to take things one step at a time, without the pressure to achieve perfection.

Today, set realistic expectations for yourself. Reflect on your current goals and responsibilities, and adjust them if needed to better align with your well-being. Understand that it's okay to prioritize your health and happiness over unrealistic demands.

Words of Wisdom: "Progress, not perfection, is what we should be asking of ourselves." —Julia Cameron

From the Bible: "Love does not work evil to one's neighbor; therefore, love is the law's fulfillment." —Romans 13:10

Reflection Question: How can you adjust your expectations today to be more compassionate and realistic towards yourself?

March 25th: Nurture Relationships with Compassion

Our relationships are a reflection of how we treat ourselves. When we practice self-compassion, we are better equipped to extend that same kindness and understanding to others. Nurturing relationships with compassion begins with how we communicate, how we listen, and how we support one another.

Today, focus on nurturing your relationships with compassion. Be patient and understanding with those around you, and approach your interactions with an open heart. Remember, the way you treat others often mirrors the way you treat yourself, so let kindness and compassion guide your words and actions.

Words of Wisdom: "Compassion for others begins with kindness to ourselves." —Pema Chodron

From the Bible: "With all humility and mildness, with patience, putting up with one another in love." —Ephesians 4:2

Reflection Question: How can you bring more compassion into your relationships, starting with the way you treat yourself?

March 26th: Practice Deep Breathing

When life becomes overwhelming, taking a moment to breathe deeply can make all the difference. Deep breathing is a simple yet powerful tool to calm your mind and body, helping you respond to situations with greater patience and clarity. It's a form of self-compassion that allows you to pause and reset, especially when faced with stress or frustration.

Today, whenever you feel tension or impatience rising, take a few deep breaths. Allow each breath to bring you back to a place of calm and centeredness. This practice not only benefits you but also helps you respond more thoughtfully to those around you, including your children.

Words of Wisdom: "Breathing in, I calm my body. Breathing out, I smile. Dwelling in the present moment, I know this is a wonderful moment." —Thich Nhat Hanh

From the Bible: "Whoever is slow to anger has great discernment, but one who is impatient exalts foolishness." —Proverbs 14:29

Reflection Question: How can deep breathing help you cultivate more patience and self-compassion in your daily life, especially in challenging moments?

March 27th: Encourage Independence in Children

Encouraging independence in your children is an act of love that requires patience and trust. It means allowing them to try new things on their own, even if it takes longer or isn't done perfectly. This not only builds their confidence but also teaches them valuable life skills. As you encourage your children's independence, remember to be patient with their learning process, just as you are with your own growth.

Today, support your children in trying something new on their own. Whether it's a task at home or a new skill, give them the space to explore and learn. Celebrate their efforts, knowing that your patience is helping them grow into capable individuals.

Words of Wisdom: "The greatest gifts you can give your children are the roots of responsibility and the wings of independence." —Denis Waitley

From the Bible: "Continue putting up with one another and forgiving one another freely even if anyone has a cause for complaint against another. Just as Jehovah freely forgave you, you must also do the same." —Colossians 3:13

Reflection Question: How can you practice patience and self-compassion as you support your children's journey toward independence?

March 28th: Listen Actively

Active listening is a powerful way to show compassion, both to yourself and to others. When you listen attentively, you create a space where understanding and connection can flourish. This is especially important in your relationships with your children, as it helps them feel valued and heard. By practicing active listening, you also nurture your own sense of patience and presence.

Today, focus on actively listening to your children and loved ones. Give them your full attention, without interrupting or planning your response. This practice not only strengthens your relationships but also helps you cultivate patience and empathy.

Words of Wisdom: "Most people do not listen with the intent to understand; they listen with the intent to reply." —Stephen R. Covey

From the Bible: "The one slow to anger is better than a mighty man, and the one controlling his temper than one conquering a city." —Proverbs 16:32

Reflection Question: How can active listening enhance your relationships and deepen your practice of self-compassion?

March 29th: Maintain a Calm Demeanor

Children often mirror the emotions of the adults around them. By maintaining a calm demeanor, especially in stressful situations, you not only model patience for your children but also create a more peaceful environment at home. This practice is a form of self-compassion, as it allows you to stay grounded and respond to challenges with grace.

Today, practice maintaining a calm demeanor in your interactions with others, especially your children. When faced with stress or conflict, take a moment to center yourself before responding. Your calmness will help to diffuse tension and promote a sense of peace.

Words of Wisdom: "Peace begins with a smile." —Mother Teresa

From the Bible: "A mild answer turns away rage, but a harsh word stirs up anger." —Proverbs 15:1

Reflection Question: How can maintaining a calm demeanor help you nurture a more peaceful and compassionate environment for yourself and your children?

March 30th: Set Realistic Expectations for Yourself and Your Children

Setting realistic expectations is a vital part of self-compassion. Recognizing your own limits and those of your children allows you to approach life with patience and understanding. It's important to remember that growth, whether in yourself or your children, is a gradual process that unfolds over time. By setting achievable goals and being patient with the process, you create a nurturing environment that encourages progress without the burden of unrealistic demands.

Today, take a moment to reassess the expectations you've set for yourself and your children. Ensure that they are realistic and conducive to well-being. Embrace the journey, knowing that it's okay to take things one step at a time. This approach not only reduces stress but also fosters a sense of accomplishment and growth.

Words of Wisdom: "It is not the mountain we conquer, but ourselves." —Sir Edmund Hillary

From the Bible: "Hatred is what stirs up contentions, but love covers all offenses." —Proverbs 10:12

Reflection Question: How can adjusting your expectations to be more realistic and compassionate help you and your children grow with patience and confidence?

April – Cultivating Inner Strength

April is a month of transformation, where the gentle whispers of spring encourage us to dig deep and find the strength within. As nature begins to bloom, it's a reminder that true growth often requires us to clear away the old, forgive ourselves and others, embrace vulnerability, and ultimately bloom with resilience. Cultivating inner strength is not about force or rigidity, but about the quiet power that comes from knowing who you are, accepting your imperfections, and continuing to move forward with grace.

This month, we will embark on a journey of inner strength, focusing on the themes of clearing emotional clutter, planting seeds of forgiveness, embracing vulnerability, and blooming with resilience. Each week will guide you through these aspects, helping you to harness the strength that lies within, even when faced with life's challenges.

Acts of kindness, whether in your community, personal relationships, workplace, or toward yourself, will play a significant role in this process. These small gestures not only uplift others but also fortify your own spirit, reminding you that strength is found in love and compassion. As you move through April, let these acts of kindness be a testament to the inner strength you are cultivating—a strength that allows you to live in harmony with the rhythms of life, to embrace uncertainty with openness, and to co-create a reality filled with abundance, joy, and fulfillment.

By the end of this month, may you find yourself blooming with resilience, rooted in the knowledge that your inner strength is a source of endless possibilities.

Week 1: Clearing Emotional Clutter

Clearing emotional clutter is essential for cultivating inner strength. Just as you might declutter your home to create a more peaceful environment, clearing the emotional baggage that weighs you down opens up space for growth, joy, and compassion. This week is about letting go of old hurts, unresolved anger, and limiting beliefs that no longer serve you. By releasing these, you allow kindness and love to flow more freely in your life.

Each day this week, focus on a different aspect of emotional clutter. Reflect on past experiences that may be holding you back and consider how they've shaped your current mindset. Then, practice kindness—toward yourself and others—as you gently let go of these burdens. This might involve forgiving someone who has hurt you, releasing resentment, or simply allowing yourself to feel and process difficult emotions.

April 1st: Releasing Past Hurts

The first step in clearing emotional clutter is releasing past hurts that continue to occupy space in your heart. Holding onto old wounds prevents you from moving forward with a light and open spirit. By letting go of these pains, you create room for kindness, love, and growth.

Today, focus on releasing a hurt you've been holding onto. This could be an unresolved conflict or a lingering resentment. As an act of kindness, write a letter of forgiveness—whether to yourself or someone else—and release the burden that's been weighing you down. Even if you never send the letter, the act of writing it can be a powerful tool for healing.

Words of Wisdom: "Anger is a poison you take hoping to hurt another, but it only harms your own soul." —Wayne Dyer, *There's a Spiritual Solution to Every Problem*

From the Bible: "But if your enemy is hungry, feed him; if he is thirsty, give him something to drink, for by doing this you will heap fiery coals on his head." —Romans 12:20

Reflection Question: What past hurt can you release today, and how will letting go of it make room for more kindness and peace in your life?

April 2nd: Clearing the Mind Through Meditation

Emotional clutter often manifests as mental clutter—anxiety, overthinking, and a lack of focus. Meditation is a powerful practice that helps to clear the mind and create space for clarity and peace. By regularly meditating, you can cultivate a sense of inner calm that allows kindness to flow more freely.

Today, dedicate a few minutes to meditation. Find a quiet place where you can sit comfortably and focus on your breath. As thoughts arise, gently acknowledge them and let them pass without judgment. This practice of mindfulness helps to clear the mental clutter that often clouds your emotions.

Words of Wisdom: "The greatest weapon against stress is our ability to choose one thought over another." —William James

From the Bible: "The fruitage of the spirit is love, joy, peace, patience, kindness, goodness, faith, mildness, self-control. Against such things, there is no law." —Galatians 5:22-23

Reflection Question: How can regular meditation help you clear mental and emotional clutter, allowing you to respond to life's challenges with greater kindness and clarity?

April 3rd: Letting Go of Perfectionism

Perfectionism is a form of emotional clutter that can prevent you from experiencing true joy and contentment. It often stems from the fear of not being enough, leading to constant self-criticism and a reluctance to embrace your imperfections. Letting go of perfectionism allows you to be kinder to yourself and to others.

Today, challenge your perfectionistic tendencies by embracing your flaws and mistakes. Instead of striving for perfection, aim for progress. Celebrate small victories and be gentle with yourself when things don't go as planned. This kindness towards yourself will naturally extend to those around you.

Words of Wisdom: "The most fundamental aggression to ourselves, the most fundamental harm we can do to ourselves, is to remain ignorant by not having the courage and the respect to look at ourselves honestly and gently." — Pema Chödrön, Comfortable with Uncertainty

From the Bible: "Above all things, have intense love for one another, because love covers a multitude of sins." —1 Peter 4:8

Reflection Question: What areas of your life are you holding to unrealistic standards, and how can you practice kindness by letting go of the need for perfection?

April 4th: Simplifying Your Life

Simplifying your life is another way to clear emotional clutter. When your life is cluttered with too many commitments, possessions, or distractions, it becomes difficult to focus on what truly matters. By simplifying, you create space for kindness, gratitude, and peace to flourish.

Today, take a small step toward simplifying your life. This could be decluttering a physical space, saying "no" to an unnecessary obligation, or turning off digital distractions for a period of time. Each act of simplification is a kindness you offer yourself, allowing you to focus on what brings you true joy.

Words of Wisdom: "Simplicity is the ultimate sophistication." — Leonardo da Vinci

From the Bible: "Seek Jehovah, all you meek ones of the earth, who observe his righteous decrees. Seek righteousness, seek meekness. Probably you will be concealed on the day of Jehovah's anger." — Zephaniah 2:3

Reflection Question: What is one area of your life that you can simplify today, and how will this act of kindness towards yourself help clear emotional clutter?

April 5th: Forgiving Yourself

Self-forgiveness is a crucial part of clearing emotional clutter. Often, we hold onto guilt and regret, punishing ourselves for past mistakes. This internal burden not only hinders our growth but also blocks the flow of kindness and compassion within us. Letting go of self-blame is an act of kindness that frees you to move forward with a lighter heart.

Today, take a moment to forgive yourself for something you've been holding onto. Reflect on a past mistake, and instead of judging yourself harshly, offer yourself the same compassion you would extend to a friend. Write down what you're forgiving yourself for, and release it with love.

Words of Wisdom: "Forgive yourself for not knowing what you didn't know before you learned it." —Maya Angelou

From the Bible: "But the wisdom from above is first of all pure, then peaceable, reasonable, ready to obey, full of mercy and good fruits, impartial, not hypocritical." —James 3:17

Reflection Question: What do you need to forgive yourself for today, and how will this act of self-compassion help you clear emotional clutter?

April 6th: Releasing Expectations of Others

Holding onto rigid expectations of others can create tension and disappointment, cluttering your emotional landscape with frustration and resentment. Releasing these expectations is a form of kindness, both to yourself and to those around you. It allows you to accept people as they are, fostering healthier and more peaceful relationships.

Today, focus on releasing unrealistic expectations you may have of others. Consider where you might be holding onto disappointment because someone didn't meet your expectations. Practice letting go of these demands, and instead, approach your interactions with openness and acceptance.

Words of Wisdom: "Expectations are the root of all heartache." — William Shakespeare

From the Bible: "The kind man benefits himself, but the cruel person brings trouble on himself." —Proverbs 11:17

Reflection Question: What expectations of others can you release today to bring more peace and kindness into your relationships?

April 7th: Embracing Change with Kindness

Change is inevitable, yet it often brings discomfort and resistance. However, embracing change with kindness can transform how you experience it. Instead of fighting against the flow of life, approach changes with a mindset of compassion and curiosity. This openness allows you to grow and adapt with grace.

Today, identify a change in your life that you've been resisting. Rather than viewing it as an obstacle, try to see it as an opportunity for growth. Offer yourself kindness as you navigate this transition, acknowledging that it's okay to feel uncertain or scared. Trust that this change is part of your journey.

Words of Wisdom: "Change is not something that we should fear. Rather, it is something that we should welcome. For without change, nothing in this world would ever grow or blossom." —B.K.S. Iyengar

From the Bible: "Stop being molded by this system of things, but be transformed by making your mind over, so that you may prove to yourselves the good and acceptable and perfect will of God." — Romans 12:2

Reflection Question: How can you embrace a current change in your life with kindness, seeing it as an opportunity rather than a challenge?

Week 2: Planting Seeds of Forgiveness

Forgiveness is one of the most powerful acts of kindness you can offer— to yourself and to others. It's like planting seeds in the garden of your heart; with time, these seeds grow into the flowers of peace, healing, and freedom. Forgiveness doesn't mean condoning what happened or forgetting the hurt, but rather choosing to release the hold that past wounds have on your life. It's about clearing away the emotional clutter that comes from holding onto grudges, resentment, or guilt.

This week, we will focus on planting seeds of forgiveness. Each day, you'll be encouraged to take small steps toward letting go of past hurts, forgiving those who have wronged you, and, perhaps most importantly, forgiving yourself. By nurturing these seeds, you're not only freeing yourself from the burden of anger and pain but also creating space for new growth, joy, and connection.

April 8th: Forgiving Someone Who Hurt You

Forgiving someone who has hurt you can be one of the most challenging things to do. However, holding onto anger and resentment only weighs you down and keeps you stuck in the past. Forgiveness is a gift you give yourself, allowing you to move forward with peace and clarity. It's about releasing the hold that the pain has on your heart, not about excusing the behavior.

Today, reflect on someone who has hurt you and consider what it would mean to forgive them. Imagine planting a seed of forgiveness in your heart, allowing it to grow and transform your pain into peace. You might not be ready to forgive entirely, but even the intention to forgive is a powerful step forward.

Words of Wisdom: "Forgiveness is giving up the hope that the past could have been any different." —Oprah Winfrey

From the Bible: "If, then, there is any encouragement in Christ, if any consolation of love, if any spiritual fellowship, if any tender affection and compassion, make my joy full by being of the same mind and having the same love, being completely united, having the one thought in mind." —Philippians 2:1-2

Reflection Question: What would it take for you to begin the process of forgiving someone who has hurt you, and how can this act of kindness towards yourself free you from the past?

April 9th: Forgiving Yourself for Past Mistakes

Self-forgiveness is often the hardest form of forgiveness to extend. We can be our own worst critics, holding onto guilt and shame long after we've made a mistake. But just as you would offer forgiveness to a friend, it's important to offer that same kindness to yourself. Remember, you are human, and mistakes are part of the journey.

Today, focus on forgiving yourself for a past mistake. Reflect on what happened, acknowledge the lesson learned, and then release the guilt you've been carrying. You deserve to move forward with a lighter heart, free from the burden of self-judgment.

Words of Wisdom: "To forgive is to set a prisoner free and discover that the prisoner was you." —Lewis B. Smedes

From the Bible: "By loyal love and faithfulness, error is atoned for, and by the fear of Jehovah, one turns away from bad." —Proverbs 16:6

Reflection Question: What past mistake do you need to forgive yourself for, and how can this act of self-compassion help you move forward with greater peace?

April 10th: Letting Go of Grudges

Grudges are like weeds in the garden of your heart; they choke out the flowers of joy and peace. Holding onto a grudge might feel justified, but in the long run, it only causes more harm to you than to anyone else. Letting go of grudges is an act of kindness that frees you to experience life with a lighter, more open heart.

Today, identify a grudge you've been holding onto and make the conscious choice to let it go. This doesn't mean forgetting what happened or ignoring your feelings—it means choosing not to let the grudge control your emotions any longer. Allow this act of forgiveness to clear away the weeds and make room for new growth.

Words of Wisdom: "What you think, you create. What you feel, you attract. What you imagine, you become." — Rhonda Byrne, The Power

From the Bible: "Finally, all of you be like-minded, showing fellow feeling, having brotherly affection, tenderly compassionate, humble in mind." —1 Peter 3:8

Reflection Question: What grudge can you release today, and how will letting go of it help you cultivate more kindness and peace in your life?

April 11th: Practicing Forgiveness in Everyday Moments

Forgiveness doesn't always have to be about big, life-changing events. It can also be practiced in the small, everyday moments—when someone cuts you off in traffic, when a friend says something hurtful, or when a coworker makes a mistake. These are opportunities to practice forgiveness in real-time, choosing kindness over anger.

Today, practice forgiveness in the small moments. When something irritates you or when someone wrongs you in a minor way, take a deep breath and choose to let it go. Each time you do this, you're planting seeds of forgiveness that will grow into a more compassionate and resilient heart.

Words of Wisdom: "In forgiving, you reclaim your power and embrace the love that transcends all hurt." —Dr. Joe Dispenza, *Becoming Supernatural*

From the Bible: "Finally, all of you, be like-minded, be sympathetic, love one another, be compassionate and humble." —1 Peter 3:8

Reflection Question: How can you practice forgiveness in the small, everyday moments of life, and how does this contribute to your overall sense of peace and well-being?

April 12th: Forgiving with Compassion

Forgiveness isn't just about letting go of anger; it's also about approaching the situation with compassion. When you forgive someone, you're choosing to see them as a fellow human being who, like you, is imperfect and capable of making mistakes. This act of compassion softens the heart and opens the door to deeper understanding and healing.

Today, when you think about someone you need to forgive, try to see the situation from their perspective. Offer them compassion, recognizing that they may have been acting out of their own pain or confusion. This doesn't excuse their behavior, but it does allow you to release anger and embrace a more peaceful mindset.

Words of Wisdom: "Compassion and forgiveness are not luxuries; they are necessities. Without them, humanity cannot survive." —Dalai Lama

From the Bible: "Keep on loving one another as brothers. Do not forget hospitality, for through it some unknowingly entertained angels." —Hebrews 13:1-2

Reflection Question: How can approaching forgiveness with compassion help you heal and bring more kindness into your interactions with others?

April 13th: Acts of Kindness as a Path to Forgiveness

Sometimes, the best way to forgive is through action. Acts of kindness, even small ones, can help to bridge the gap between you and someone you need to forgive. By choosing to be kind, you're actively dismantling the barriers that resentment and anger have built, allowing forgiveness to take root in your heart.

Today, choose an act of kindness to extend to someone you need to forgive. This could be as simple as sending a kind message, offering a compliment, or helping them in some way. Let this act of kindness be a step toward forgiveness, allowing you to release the burden of negativity and move forward with a lighter heart.

Words of Wisdom: "Every act of kindness ripples through the universe, creating waves of love and connection." —Rhonda Byrne, *The Power*

From the Bible: "Righteousness is what guards the blameless one, but wickedness overthrows the sinner." —Proverbs 13:6

Reflection Question: What small act of kindness can you offer today as a step toward forgiveness, and how might this action help heal the relationship?

April 14th: Forgiving Yourself for Not Being Perfect

We often hold ourselves to impossibly high standards, expecting perfection in everything we do. But this expectation can lead to self-criticism and a lack of self-compassion. Forgiving yourself for not being perfect is an act of kindness that allows you to embrace your humanity and grow from your experiences.

Today, reflect on an area of your life where you've been hard on yourself. Acknowledge that it's okay to make mistakes and that perfection isn't the goal. Forgive yourself for any perceived shortcomings and offer yourself the same kindness you would extend to a friend.

Words of Wisdom: "Perfectionism is self-abuse of the highest order." —Anne Wilson Schaef

From the Bible: "Whoever does not love has not come to know God, because God is love." —1 John 4:8

Reflection Question: In what ways can you practice self-forgiveness today, and how will this act of kindness help you grow in self-compassion and resilience?

Week 3: Embracing Vulnerability

Vulnerability is often seen as a weakness, but in reality, it is one of the greatest strengths we possess. As women, we are taught to be strong, to hold it all together, and to carry the weight of the world on our shoulders. But true strength lies in the courage to be vulnerable—to share our hearts, to ask for help, and to let others see us as we truly are.

This week, we'll focus on embracing vulnerability as a pathway to deeper connection and self-awareness. Vulnerability allows us to strip away the layers of armor we've built up over time, revealing our true selves. It's in these raw, honest moments that we find our greatest strength and our deepest connections with others.

Allow yourself to be seen, to be heard, and to be loved exactly as you are. Embrace the power of vulnerability, and watch as it transforms your relationships, your self-perception, and your life. This week, let's walk this path together, with hearts open and spirits ready to embrace all that we are.

April 15th: The Courage to Be Seen

Being truly seen by others can feel like one of the scariest things we do. It means showing up as we are, without the masks or the shields we often hide behind. Yet, it is in these moments of authenticity that real connections are forged. When we allow ourselves to be seen, we give others permission to do the same, creating a space of mutual trust and understanding.

Today, take a step toward allowing yourself to be seen. Share something real and vulnerable with someone you trust—a fear, a dream, or a feeling you've been keeping inside. This act of opening up is an expression of kindness towards yourself, as it releases the burden of carrying everything alone, and towards others, as it invites them into your true self.

Words of Wisdom: "Vulnerability is not winning or losing; it's having the courage to show up and be seen when we have no control over the outcome." —Brené Brown

From the Bible: "So, then, let us pursue the things making for peace and the things that build one another up." —Romans 14:19

Reflection Question: What part of yourself can you share today to embrace vulnerability and deepen your connections with others?

April 16th: The Strength in Asking for Help

Asking for help is a brave act of vulnerability. It acknowledges that we don't have to do everything on our own and that seeking support is a natural and necessary part of life. Often, the hardest part of asking for help is overcoming the fear of being seen as weak or inadequate. But in truth, reaching out is a sign of strength and self-compassion.

Today, practice kindness towards yourself by asking for help with something you've been struggling with. Whether it's reaching out to a friend, family member, or colleague, allow yourself to receive the support you need. This act of vulnerability not only helps you but also strengthens your relationships by fostering trust and collaboration.

Words of Wisdom: "Asking for help is not a sign of weakness; it's a sign of strength." —Michelle Obama

From the Bible: "Above all things, have intense love for one another, because love covers a multitude of sins." —1 Peter 4:8

Reflection Question: In what area of your life do you need help, and how can asking for support be an act of kindness towards yourself and those around you?

April 17th: Embracing Emotional Honesty

Vulnerability requires emotional honesty—not just with others, but with ourselves. It's about acknowledging what we truly feel, rather than suppressing or denying our emotions. When we embrace emotional honesty, we allow ourselves to heal and grow, and we create deeper, more authentic connections with those around us.

Today, practice emotional honesty by acknowledging and expressing your true feelings. Whether you're feeling joy, sadness, anger, or fear, give yourself permission to feel and express these emotions. Share your feelings with someone you trust, or write them down in a journal. This act of vulnerability is a kindness to yourself, as it honors your truth and allows you to move through your emotions with compassion.

Words of Wisdom: "Emotional honesty opens the door to emotional freedom." —John C. Maxwell

From the Bible: "Continue putting up with one another and forgiving one another freely even if anyone has a cause for complaint against another. Just as Jehovah freely forgave you, you must also do the same." —Colossians 3:13

Reflection Question: How can you practice emotional honesty today, and how might this act of vulnerability bring more kindness and authenticity into your life?

April 18th: Finding Strength in Sharing Your Story

Sharing your story is one of the most powerful ways to connect with others. It's an act of vulnerability that requires you to open up about your experiences, both the highs and the lows. By sharing your story, you not only free yourself from the weight of carrying it alone but also offer others the opportunity to learn from and connect with your journey.

Today, consider sharing a part of your story with someone who might benefit from hearing it. Whether it's a story of struggle, triumph, or something in between, your experiences have the power to inspire and uplift others. This act of kindness not only strengthens your own resilience but also builds a bridge of understanding and empathy between you and those you share with.

Words of Wisdom: "Your deepest truth, when expressed, becomes a source of liberation and transformation." —Pema Chodron, *Comfortable with Uncertainty*

From the Bible: "Hate what is bad, and love what is good, and establish justice in the gate. It may be that Jehovah the God of armies will show favor to the remaining ones of Joseph." —Amos 5:15

Reflection Question: What part of your story can you share today, and how might this act of vulnerability help both you and those who hear it?

April 19th: Embracing Imperfection

One of the greatest acts of vulnerability is accepting our imperfections. We often strive for perfection in our lives, but the truth is, our imperfections are what make us uniquely beautiful. Embracing your flaws, mistakes, and shortcomings with kindness allows you to live more authentically and frees you from the pressure of trying to be something you're not.

Today, practice kindness by embracing your imperfections. Reflect on an area of your life where you've been particularly hard on yourself. Instead of criticizing, offer yourself understanding and compassion. Remember, it's your imperfections that make you relatable and human.

Words of Wisdom: "There is a crack in everything, that's how the light gets in." —Leonard Cohen

From the Bible: "Let all your things take place with love." —1 Corinthians 16:14

Reflection Question: How can you embrace your imperfections today and show yourself kindness in the process?

April 20th: Vulnerability in Forgiveness

Forgiving someone requires vulnerability because it means letting go of the pain and opening your heart to healing. It's a process that involves acknowledging your hurt and then choosing to release it. Forgiveness is not about excusing the wrong, but about freeing yourself from the emotional burden it carries.

Today, consider forgiving someone who has hurt you. This doesn't mean forgetting what happened, but rather, allowing yourself to move forward without carrying the weight of resentment. Approach this act of forgiveness with kindness, both towards the person you're forgiving and towards yourself.

Words of Wisdom: "Forgiveness is the fragrance that the violet sheds on the heel that has crushed it." —Mark Twain

From the Bible: "Let your reasonableness be known to all men. The Lord is near." —Philippians 4:5

Reflection Question: How can the act of forgiving someone today bring more kindness and peace into your life?

April 21st: The Power of Admitting When You're Wrong

Admitting when you're wrong is an act of vulnerability that takes great strength. It's not easy to acknowledge our mistakes, especially when pride gets in the way. However, owning up to your errors is a powerful act of kindness that can heal relationships and deepen connections. It shows others that you value truth and integrity over ego.

Today, if you've made a mistake or hurt someone, take the brave step of admitting it. Apologize sincerely and without excuses. This act of vulnerability not only repairs the relationship but also fosters mutual respect and understanding.

Words of Wisdom: "It takes courage to say you were wrong. Admitting mistakes is a path to wisdom." —Wayne Dyer

From the Bible: "Therefore, openly confess your sins to one another and pray for one another, so that you may be healed." —James 5:16

Reflection Question: How can admitting when you're wrong and offering a sincere apology strengthen your relationships and show kindness to others and yourself?

Week 4: Blooming with Resilience

Resilience is the ability to bounce back from life's challenges, to grow through adversity, and to emerge stronger on the other side. It's not about avoiding difficulties, but about facing them with courage, kindness, and a determination to thrive. This week, we'll focus on how resilience allows us to bloom even in the toughest of circumstances, transforming pain into strength and setbacks into opportunities for growth.

This week, let's explore how small acts of kindness can help us build resilience. Whether it's offering support to someone else, showing compassion to ourselves, or simply being a positive presence in the lives of those around us, kindness is the key to unlocking our resilient spirit. As we nurture ourselves and others with kindness, we lay the foundation for a life that blooms with beauty, no matter the circumstances.

April 22nd: The Strength in Small Acts of Kindness

Resilience is built in the small moments—the tiny acts of kindness that might seem insignificant but can make a world of difference. These small gestures create ripples of positivity that help us and those around us to keep going, even when times are tough.

Today, commit to performing small acts of kindness throughout your day. Whether it's offering a compliment, holding the door open for someone, or sending a thoughtful message, these small acts can strengthen your own resilience and brighten someone else's day.

Words of Wisdom: "No act of kindness, no matter how small, is ever wasted." —Aesop

From the Bible: "Let your reasonableness become known to all men. The Lord is near." —Philippians 4:5

Reflection Question: How can small acts of kindness help you build resilience, and how might these acts positively impact those around you?

April 23rd: Bouncing Back with Compassion

Resilience isn't about never falling down; it's about how we rise after we've fallen. Compassion, both towards ourselves and others, is essential in this process. When we treat ourselves with kindness after a setback, we allow ourselves the space to heal and recover. This self-compassion helps us to bounce back stronger and more determined.

Today, reflect on a recent setback or challenge. Instead of criticizing yourself for any perceived failure, practice self-compassion. Speak to yourself with the same kindness you would offer a friend in a similar situation. This act of kindness will strengthen your resilience and help you move forward with renewed energy.

Words of Wisdom: "Too often we underestimate the power of a touch, a smile, a kind word, a listening ear, an honest compliment, or the smallest act of caring, all of which have the potential to turn a life around." —Leo Buscaglia

From the Bible: "Love is patient and kind. Love is not jealous. It does not brag, does not get puffed up." —1 Corinthians 13:4

Reflection Question: How can practicing self-compassion help you bounce back from challenges and strengthen your resilience?

April 24th: Resilience Through Community

Building resilience is not something we do alone. It's through our connections with others that we find the strength to keep going, even in the face of adversity. Acts of kindness within our community—whether it's offering support, sharing a meal, or simply being present—can create a network of resilience that lifts everyone up.

Today, focus on building resilience through your community. Reach out to someone who might need support or encouragement. Offer your time, a listening ear, or a helping hand. This act of kindness not only strengthens your own resilience but also contributes to a stronger, more connected community.

Words of Wisdom: "You cannot do a kindness too soon, for you never know how soon it will be too late." —Ralph Waldo Emerson

From the Bible: "The result of humility and the fear of Jehovah is riches and honor and life." —Proverbs 22:4

Reflection Question: How can you contribute to your community's resilience through acts of kindness, and how does this support your own growth?

April 25th: Blooming in Adversity

Just as flowers bloom in the harshest conditions, so too can we find the strength to thrive in adversity. Resilience is about using our challenges as fuel for growth, allowing us to bloom even when the odds seem stacked against us. By approaching adversity with kindness, both towards ourselves and others, we transform obstacles into opportunities for beauty and growth.

Today, reflect on a time when you faced adversity and came out stronger. What helped you to bloom in that situation? Consider how you can apply those lessons to current or future challenges. Approach your current struggles with kindness, trusting that you have the resilience to grow through them.

Words of Wisdom: "I've learned that people will forget what you said, people will forget what you did, but people will never forget how you made them feel." —Maya Angelou

From the Bible: "But let justice flow like waters, and righteousness like an ever-flowing stream." —Amos 5:24

Reflection Question: How can you use your experiences of adversity to help you bloom, and how can kindness guide you through your current challenges?

April 26th: Resilience Through Patience

Resilience often requires patience—waiting for the right time, trusting the process, and allowing things to unfold as they should. Patience is a form of kindness, both towards ourselves and others, as it gives us the space to grow without pressure or haste. When we practice patience, we build resilience by learning to endure, adapt, and remain hopeful.

Today, focus on practicing patience in a challenging situation. Whether it's waiting for something to happen, dealing with a difficult person, or working towards a long-term goal, approach it with a mindset of kindness and trust. Remember, resilience is built in these moments of patience and perseverance.

Words of Wisdom: "The moment in front of you is not bothering you. You are bothering yourself about the moment in front of you." — Michael Singer

From the Bible: "The fruitage of the spirit is love, joy, peace, patience, kindness, goodness, faith, mildness, self-control. Against such things, there is no law." —Galatians 5:22-23

Reflection Question: How can practicing patience today help you build resilience and approach your challenges with kindness?

April 27th: Finding Joy in Small Victories

Resilience isn't just about overcoming major challenges; it's also about celebrating the small victories along the way. Each step forward, no matter how small, is a testament to your strength and perseverance. Finding joy in these moments is a powerful act of kindness towards yourself, as it acknowledges your efforts and encourages continued growth.

Today, celebrate a small victory in your life. It could be completing a task, overcoming a minor obstacle, or simply making it through the day with a positive attitude. Take a moment to recognize and appreciate your progress, no matter how modest it may seem.

Words of Wisdom: "The more you praise and celebrate your life, the more there is in life to celebrate." —Oprah Winfrey

From the Bible: "During all their distress it was distressing to him. And his own personal messenger saved them. In his love and compassion, he repurchased them, and he lifted them up and carried them all the days of old." —Isaiah 63:9

Reflection Question: What small victory can you celebrate today, and how does acknowledging it help you build resilience and maintain a positive outlook?

April 28th: Kindness as a Foundation for Resilience

At the core of resilience lies kindness—kindness that nurtures, heals, and inspires. When we approach our challenges with a kind heart, we build a strong foundation for resilience. This kindness not only helps us to cope with difficulties but also enables us to lift others up as we rise.

Today, let kindness guide your actions and decisions. Whether you're dealing with a personal challenge or supporting someone else, choose to act with compassion and empathy. Let your kindness be the strength that carries you and others through difficult times.

Words of Wisdom: "Be kind whenever possible. It is always possible." —Dalai Lama

From the Bible: "Accordingly, as God's chosen ones, holy and loved, clothe yourselves with the tender affections of compassion, kindness, humility, mildness, and patience." —Colossians 3:12

Reflection Question: How can you use kindness as a foundation for resilience in your life and in the lives of those around you?

April 29th: Reflecting on Growth and Transformation

As you near the end of this month of resilience, take time to reflect on your journey. Consider the ways in which you've grown, the challenges you've overcome, and the strength you've discovered within yourself. Reflection is an act of kindness that allows you to acknowledge your progress and honor the path you've walked.

Today, spend some time reflecting on the growth and transformation you've experienced this month. Write down your thoughts, feelings, and lessons learned. This reflection will help you solidify your resilience and prepare you for future challenges with a sense of confidence and self-compassion.

Words of Wisdom: "Growth is painful. Change is painful. But nothing is as painful as staying stuck somewhere you don't belong." —N.R. Narayana Murthy

From the Bible: "The one who pursues righteousness and loyal love will find life, righteousness, and glory." —Proverbs 21:21

Reflection Question: How have you grown and transformed this month, and how can you carry these lessons of resilience forward into the future?

April 30th: Blooming Into Your True Self

After a month of focusing on resilience, you've likely discovered new strengths, developed deeper compassion, and cultivated a kinder, more resilient heart. Now, it's time to bloom into your true self—embracing all that you are and all that you've become. This final day is about celebrating your journey and stepping into the fullness of who you are with confidence and grace.

Today, take time to celebrate who you've become. Reflect on the challenges you've faced and the resilience you've built. Acknowledge your growth and embrace your true self with kindness and love. You are blooming, and your resilience is the flower that continues to grow stronger with each passing day.

Words of Wisdom: "And the day came when the risk to remain tight in a bud was more painful than the risk it took to blossom." —Anaïs Nin

From the Bible: "He has told you, O man, what is good. And what is Jehovah requiring of you? Only to exercise justice, to cherish loyalty, and to walk in modesty with your God!" —Micah 6:8

Reflection Question: How can you embrace your true self today, celebrating the resilience and strength you've cultivated throughout this month?

May: Connecting with Nature and Self

As we step into May, we turn our focus to the profound connection between personal well-being and the natural world. Nature, with its cycles of rebirth and renewal, offers us a powerful metaphor for our own growth and transformation. This month, we explore how engaging with the beauty of the natural world can inspire personal renewal and bring joy into our lives.

Spending time in nature helps us reconnect with our inner selves, providing a sense of peace and grounding. The sights, sounds, and rhythms of the natural environment remind us of life's simple pleasures and the continuous cycle of growth and renewal. Each day's devotion will guide you in drawing inspiration from nature to enhance your personal well-being and spiritual growth.

Embrace this opportunity to step outside, breathe in the fresh air, and let the natural world rejuvenate your spirit. Together, we will discover how connecting with nature can lead to a deeper connection with ourselves, fostering a sense of inner peace and joy.

Week 1: Grounding in the Present Moment

Grounding yourself in the present moment is a powerful way to connect deeply with both nature and your inner self. This week, we focus on mindfulness and being fully present, allowing the natural world to guide us toward a greater sense of peace and clarity. Just as spring brings new life and growth, practicing mindfulness helps us appreciate the beauty of each moment and fosters inner renewal.

May 1st: Embracing the Present

Spring's vibrant renewal invites us to embrace the present moment fully. Today, focus on practicing mindfulness to connect with the here and now. Step outside and notice the details around you—the blooming flowers, the chirping birds, the gentle breeze.

Take a moment to sit quietly in nature. Close your eyes, take deep breaths, and pay attention to the sensations in your body. Feel the ground beneath you, the air on your skin, and the sounds around you. Let nature's presence anchor you in the present.

In your journal, write about how this mindful practice makes you feel. Reflect on the sense of peace and clarity it brings, and commit to incorporating mindfulness into your daily routine.

Words of Wisdom: "Mindfulness is the practice of being in the present moment, fully aware of your thoughts and actions without judgment." - Thich Nhat Hanh

From the Bible: "I have calmed and quieted my soul, like a weaned child with its mother." —Psalm 131:2

Reflection Question: How can you embrace the present moment today, and what benefits do you notice from this practice?

May 2nd: Mindful Walking

Springtime is perfect for mindful walking, a practice that enhances your connection to nature and your inner self. Today, take a walk outdoors, focusing on being fully present with each step.

As you walk, notice the sights, sounds, and smells around you. Feel the ground beneath your feet and the rhythm of your breath. If your mind starts to wander, gently bring your attention back to your surroundings.

Mindful walking helps clear your mind and brings a sense of calm. Let nature guide you to a place of inner peace, appreciating the beauty of the present moment.

Words of Wisdom: "The best way to capture moments is to pay attention. This is how we cultivate mindfulness." - Jon Kabat-Zinn

From the Bible: "Go on walking in love, just as the Christ also loved us." —Ephesians 5:2

Reflection Question: How does mindful walking help you connect with nature and your inner self?

May 3rd: Nature's Sounds

Listening to the sounds of nature is a powerful way to ground yourself in the present. Today, spend time outdoors, focusing on the natural sounds around you.

Find a quiet spot and close your eyes. Listen to the birds singing, the wind rustling the leaves, and any other ambient sounds. Allow these natural melodies to bring you into the moment.

This practice helps quiet the mind and fosters a deep sense of peace. Embrace the symphony of nature as a tool for mindfulness, letting it guide you to a place of calm and clarity.

Words of Wisdom: "Nature's music is never over; her silences are pauses, not conclusions." - Mary Webb

From the Bible: "Day after day they pour forth speech; night after night they reveal knowledge." —Psalm 19:2

Reflection Question: What natural sounds bring you the most peace, and how can they help you stay grounded in the present?

May 4th: Breathing with Nature

Spring is a time of fresh air and renewal. Today, focus on your breath as a way to connect with nature and stay grounded in the present.

Find a comfortable spot outdoors and take deep, deliberate breaths. Inhale the fresh spring air, filling your lungs completely, and then exhale slowly, releasing any tension. Synchronize your breathing with the natural rhythms around you.

Breathing mindfully in nature helps you stay centered and calm. Let the purity of the air and the vitality of the season refresh your mind and spirit.

Words of Wisdom: "Mindfulness isn't difficult; we just need to remember to do it." – Sharon Salzberg

From the Bible: "The spirit of God has made me, and the breath of the Almighty gives me life." —Job 33:4

Reflection Question: How does mindful breathing in nature enhance your sense of peace and presence?

May 5th: Observing Growth

Spring is a season of visible growth and transformation. Today, focus on observing the growth around you as a way to stay present and connected to nature.

Take a walk and notice the new leaves, flowers, and budding plants. Pay attention to the small details of growth and change. Reflect on how this natural renewal mirrors your own personal growth.

Observing nature's transformation helps you appreciate the beauty of change and the importance of staying grounded in the present. Let the growth around you inspire your own journey of renewal.

Words of Wisdom: "Nature always wears the colors of the spirit." – Ralph Waldo Emerson

From the Bible: "For look! the winter has passed; the rain is over and gone. The blossoms have appeared in the land." —Song of Solomon 2:11-12

Reflection Question: What new growth in nature inspires you, and how does it reflect your own personal transformation?

May 6th: Touching the Earth

Physical contact with the earth can ground you in the present moment. Today, focus on tactile experiences with nature to enhance your mindfulness.

Spend time gardening, walking barefoot on grass, or simply touching trees and plants. Feel the textures, temperatures, and sensations of the earth beneath your fingers and toes.

Engaging with nature physically helps anchor your mind and body, bringing a sense of calm and connection. Let the simple act of touching the earth remind you of your place in the natural world.

Words of Wisdom: "To forget how to dig the earth and to tend the soil is to forget ourselves." - Mahatma Gandhi

From the Bible: "And Jehovah God formed the man out of dust from the ground and breathed into his nostrils the breath of life, and the man became a living person." —Genesis 2:7

Reflection Question: How does physical contact with nature help you feel more grounded and present?

May 7th: Mindful Reflection in Nature

Nature provides a perfect backdrop for reflection. Today, find a peaceful outdoor spot and take time to reflect mindfully on your thoughts and feelings.

Sit quietly and let your mind wander, observing your thoughts without judgment. Notice how being in nature influences your reflections and brings clarity.

Mindful reflection in nature helps you connect deeply with your inner self. Allow the natural surroundings to inspire a sense of peace and understanding.

Words of Wisdom: "Adopt the pace of nature: her secret is patience."
- Ralph Waldo Emerson

From the Bible: "He turns a desert into a pool of water, a parched land into springs of water." —Psalm 107:35

Reflection Question: How does reflecting in nature help you connect with your inner self and gain clarity?

Week 2: Flowing with Life's Changes

Spring is a season of dynamic change and renewal, reflecting the natural cycles of life. This week, we focus on flowing with life's changes, embracing adaptability and openness as we navigate the ever-shifting landscape of our lives. Just as nature adapts and thrives with each new season, we too can find joy and growth in the changes that come our way.

Adapting to change can be challenging, but it also brings opportunities for discovery and alignment with our true selves. This week's devotions will guide you in embracing change with a positive mindset, seeing each new development as a chance to grow and flourish. By flowing with life's changes, you'll learn to find joy in the journey and trust in the natural rhythms of life.

May 8th: Embracing Change with Openness

Spring's ever-changing landscape invites us to embrace change with openness and curiosity. Today, focus on viewing life's changes as opportunities for growth and discovery.

Reflect on a recent change in your life. Instead of resisting it, try to see it as a new beginning. Consider the possibilities that this change brings and how it might align with your personal growth.

Take a moment to appreciate the flexibility and resilience you've shown in the past. Remind yourself that just like nature, you have the ability to adapt and thrive.

Words of Wisdom: "Change is the only constant in life. One's ability to adapt to those changes will determine your success in life." - Benjamin Franklin

From the Bible: "A person's steps are directed by Jehovah. How can anyone understand his own way?" —Proverbs 20:24

Reflection Question: How can you embrace a recent change in your life with openness and curiosity, seeing it as an opportunity for growth?

May 9th: Finding Joy in New Beginnings

Change often brings new beginnings that can be exciting and filled with potential. Today, focus on finding joy in the fresh starts that change offers.

Think about a recent new beginning in your life. Reflect on the positive aspects of this change and the opportunities it presents. Embrace the excitement of starting something new, and let go of any fear or anxiety associated with it.

Celebrate this new beginning by taking a small step forward. Whether it's starting a new project, meeting new people, or exploring a new interest, find joy in the process of beginning anew.

Words of Wisdom: "Each new beginning is a place to start anew; it's from the ending that we find a new beginning." – Lao Tzu

From the Bible: "And He will wipe out every tear from their eyes, and death will be no more, neither will mourning nor outcry nor pain be anymore." —Revelation 21:4

Reflection Question: What new beginning can you celebrate today, and how can you find joy in the opportunities it brings?

May 10th: Adapting with Grace

Gracefully adapting to change is a skill that can be cultivated. Today, focus on how you can approach changes in your life with grace and poise.

Identify a change you are currently experiencing. Consider how you can adapt to this change in a positive and constructive way. Practice patience and self-compassion as you navigate this transition.

Recognize that adapting with grace involves being kind to yourself and others. Accept that it's okay to feel uncertain and that you can take things one step at a time.

Words of Wisdom: Adaptability is about the powerful difference between adapting to cope and adapting to win." – Max McKeown

From the Bible: "Jehovah will accomplish what concerns me. Your loyal love, O Jehovah, endures forever." —Psalm 138:8

Reflection Question: How can you adapt to a current change in your life with grace and patience, allowing yourself to grow through the process?

May 11th: Learning from Nature's Cycles

Nature's cycles teach us about the inevitability of change and the beauty that comes with it. Today, focus on learning from nature's example of continuous renewal and transformation.

Spend time observing the natural world around you. Notice the cycles of growth, blooming, and renewal. Reflect on how these natural cycles mirror the changes in your own life.

Let nature's resilience inspire you to embrace your own cycles of change. Trust that, like nature, you have the ability to adapt, renew, and flourish through life's transitions.

Words of Wisdom: "To walk into nature is to witness a thousand miracles." – Mary Davis

From the Bible: "The green grass dries up, the blossom withers, but the word of our God endures forever." —Isaiah 40:8

Reflection Question: What can you learn from observing nature's cycles, and how can these lessons help you embrace changes in your life?

May 12th: Trusting the Process

Change often requires us to trust the process, even when the outcome is uncertain. Today, focus on building trust in the journey and the natural unfolding of events.

Think about a change you are going through that feels uncertain. Reflect on past experiences where trusting the process led to positive outcomes. Remind yourself that patience and faith are essential in navigating change.

Practice letting go of the need to control every aspect of the change. Trust that the process will lead you to where you need to be, and embrace the journey with confidence and hope.

Words of Wisdom: "To understand change, you must plunge into it, move with it, and join the dance." – Alan Watts

From the Bible: "You will safeguard those who fully lean on you; You will give them continuous peace, because it is in you that they trust." — Isaiah 26:3

Reflection Question: How can you build trust in the process of change, and what positive outcomes can you anticipate from embracing this trust?

May 13th: Embracing Uncertainty

Uncertainty is a natural part of life's changes. Today, focus on embracing uncertainty with a sense of curiosity and openness.

Reflect on a situation where uncertainty feels challenging. Instead of fearing the unknown, approach it with curiosity. Ask yourself what new experiences and opportunities might arise from this uncertainty.

Practice mindfulness to stay grounded in the present moment. Accept that not knowing everything is part of the journey, and find peace in being open to whatever comes next.

Words of Wisdom: "Embrace uncertainty. Some of the most beautiful chapters in our lives won't have a title until much later." - Bob Goff

From the Bible: "For we are walking by faith, not by sight." —2 Corinthians 5:7

Reflection Question: How can you embrace uncertainty with curiosity and openness, and what new opportunities might arise from this approach?

May 14th: Growing Through Change

Change is an opportunity for growth and self-discovery. Today, focus on how you can grow through the changes you are experiencing.

Think about a recent change in your life. Reflect on the personal growth it has prompted. What new skills, perspectives, or strengths have you developed as a result?

Celebrate your growth by acknowledging your progress and setting new goals. Embrace the ongoing process of learning and evolving, knowing that each change helps you become a more resilient and capable person.

Words of Wisdom: "If you are willing, change can be an opportunity for transformation rather than just a mere change of situation," — Sadhguru

From the Bible: "Moreover, we know that all things work together for good to those who love God, to those who are called according to his purpose." —Romans 8:28

Reflection Question: How have you grown through a recent change, and what new goals can you set to continue your journey of personal development?

Week 3: Reflecting on Growth and Transformation

Personal growth and transformation are continuous processes that shape who we are and how we navigate the world. This week, we focus on reflecting on our own growth, celebrating the milestones we've achieved, and appreciating the journey that has brought us here. By acknowledging our progress and the changes we've embraced, we can gain a deeper understanding of ourselves and the resilience we've developed.

Reflecting on growth allows us to recognize the strength and courage it takes to transform. It also provides an opportunity to set new intentions and goals, ensuring that we continue to evolve and thrive. This week's devotions will guide you through a series of reflections, encouraging you to celebrate your personal journey and the transformations that have brought you closer to your true self.

May 15th: Celebrating Milestones

Every milestone in your journey of growth and transformation deserves to be celebrated. Today, focus on recognizing and honoring the milestones you've achieved.

Reflect on a significant milestone in your personal growth. It could be overcoming a challenge, achieving a goal, or making a meaningful change. Take a moment to appreciate the effort and perseverance it took to reach this point.

Celebrate this milestone by acknowledging your hard work and dedication. Treat yourself to something special, share your achievement with a loved one, or simply take a moment to reflect on your success.

Words of Wisdom: "The only way to experience life fully is to be constantly willing to let go of everything you know and adapt to whatever life throws at you." — Sadhguru

From the Bible: "I will praise you, Jehovah my God, with all my heart, and I will glorify your name forever." —Psalm 86:12

Reflection Question: What significant milestone can you celebrate today, and how can you honor your journey and achievements?

May 16th: Recognizing Daily Growth

Growth isn't always about grand achievements; it often happens in small, daily increments. Today, focus on recognizing the subtle but important growth you experience each day.

Think about the small steps you've taken recently that contribute to your personal growth. It could be developing a new habit, learning something new, or making a small but positive change in your behavior.

Acknowledge these daily victories and appreciate their impact on your overall journey. Remember, every small step forward is a building block towards your larger goals.

Words of Wisdom: "Success is the progressive realization of a worthy goal or ideal." – Earl Nightingale

From the Bible: "So let us not give up in doing what is fine, for in due season we will reap if we do not tire out." —Galatians 6:9

Reflection Question: What small steps have you taken recently that contribute to your personal growth, and how can you celebrate these daily victories?

May 17th: Embracing Change

Change is a catalyst for growth and transformation. Today, focus on embracing the changes you've experienced and how they've contributed to your development.

Reflect on a recent change in your life. Consider how this change has impacted you and what you've learned from it. Embrace the transformation it has brought and recognize the positive aspects of this change.

Celebrate your ability to adapt and grow through change. Acknowledge the resilience and flexibility you've developed as a result.

Words of Wisdom: "Change is the essence of life; be willing to surrender what you are for what you could become." - Reinhold Niebuhr

From the Bible: "Keep seeking the things above, where the Christ is, seated at the right hand of God." —Colossians 3:1

Reflection Question: How has a recent change in your life contributed to your growth, and what positive transformations have you experienced?

May 18th: Learning from Challenges

Challenges are opportunities for growth and self-discovery. Today, focus on reflecting on the challenges you've faced and the lessons they've taught you.

Think about a significant challenge you've overcome. Reflect on how it tested your strength, resilience, and determination. Consider the valuable lessons you've learned from this experience.

Celebrate your ability to grow through adversity. Acknowledge the strength you've gained and the personal growth that has come from overcoming challenges.

Words of Wisdom: "The struggle you're in today is developing the strength you need for tomorrow." - Robert Tew

From the Bible: "But even if you should suffer for the sake of righteousness, you are happy." —1 Peter 3:14

Reflection Question: What significant challenge have you overcome, and what valuable lessons have you learned from this experience?

May 19th: Appreciating Personal Growth

Take time to appreciate your personal growth and the journey you've undertaken. Today, focus on recognizing how far you've come and the person you've become.

Reflect on your personal growth over the past year. Think about the goals you've achieved, the habits you've developed, and the positive changes you've made. Acknowledge the hard work and dedication it took to reach this point.

Appreciate the journey and the progress you've made. Celebrate your growth by expressing gratitude for the experiences and lessons that have shaped you.

Words of Wisdom: "Change is not just a possibility – it is a reality, it is happening all the time. If you resist change, you resist life" – Sadhguru

From the Bible: "So that you may walk worthy of Jehovah in full agreement with him, bearing fruit in every good work and increasing in the knowledge of God." —Colossians 1:10

Reflection Question: How can you appreciate your personal growth over the past year, and what aspects of your journey are you most grateful for?

May 20th: Setting New Intentions

Growth and transformation are ongoing processes. Today, focus on setting new intentions and goals for your continued personal development.

Reflect on the areas of your life where you'd like to see further growth. Consider what new goals or intentions you can set to continue your journey of transformation. Write these down and make a plan to achieve them.

Embrace the excitement of setting new intentions and the possibilities they bring. Commit to taking the necessary steps to continue your personal growth.

Words of Wisdom: "Everything is changeable, everything is transformable. If you are willing, it is possible for you to be the way you want to be." - Sadhguru

From the Bible: "May he give you the desire of your heart and cause all your plans to succeed." —Psalm 20:4

Reflection Question: What new intentions or goals can you set for your continued personal growth, and how will you work towards achieving them?

May 21st: Reflecting on Inner Transformation

Inner transformation is a deep and profound aspect of personal growth. Today, focus on reflecting on the inner changes you've experienced and how they've shaped your character and perspective.

Think about the inner transformations you've undergone. Reflect on how your thoughts, beliefs, and attitudes have evolved. Consider the positive impact these changes have had on your life and relationships.

Celebrate your inner growth and the person you've become. Recognize the strength and wisdom you've gained through your journey of inner transformation.

Words of Wisdom: "The only real journey is the one within." – Marcel Proust

From the Bible: "And all of us, while with unveiled faces we reflect like mirrors the glory of Jehovah, are being transformed into the same image from glory to glory, exactly as it is done by Jehovah the Spirit." —2 Corinthians 3:18

Reflection Question: How has your inner transformation shaped your character and perspective, and what positive changes have you experienced?

Week 4: Celebrating Inner and Outer Beauty

Beauty surrounds us, both within ourselves and in the world we live in. This week, we focus on recognizing and celebrating beauty in all its forms. By appreciating the beauty within us, we cultivate self-love and confidence. By observing the beauty around us, we find inspiration and joy. Embracing beauty helps us see the positive aspects of life and appreciate the richness of our experiences.

This week's devotions will guide you in discovering the beauty within your heart and soul, as well as in the natural world and your everyday surroundings. By celebrating beauty, you deepen your connection with yourself and the world, fostering a sense of peace and fulfillment. Let this week be a time of joy and appreciation as you open your eyes and heart to the beauty that exists all around you.

May 22nd: Recognizing Inner Beauty

Recognizing your inner beauty is an important step towards self-love and confidence. Today, focus on identifying and celebrating the qualities that make you unique and beautiful from within.

Reflect on your inner strengths and virtues. In what ways are you kind, compassionate, resilient, or creative? Take a moment to appreciate these qualities and recognize how they contribute to your overall beauty.

Celebrate your inner beauty by engaging in activities that make you feel good about yourself. Whether it's writing affirmations, meditating, or doing something you love, honor the beautiful person you are inside.

Words of Wisdom: "The power of love is the power of beauty, it makes you shine from the inside out." — The Power of Rhonda Byrne

From the Bible: "Do not let your adornment be external—the braiding of hair and the wearing of gold ornaments or fine clothing—but let it be the secret person of the heart in the incorruptible adornment of a quiet and mild spirit, which is of great value in the eyes of God." —1 Peter 3:3-4

Reflection Question: What inner qualities make you beautiful, and how can you celebrate your inner beauty today?

May 23rd: Appreciating Outer Beauty

Outer beauty is not just about appearance; it's about the grace and presence you bring into the world. Today, focus on appreciating and celebrating your outer beauty.

Reflect on what you love about your physical appearance. It could be your smile, your eyes, or the way you carry yourself. Take time to appreciate these features without comparison or criticism.

Celebrate your outer beauty by engaging in self-care practices that make you feel good about yourself. Dress in clothes that make you feel confident, take a relaxing bath, or pamper yourself with your favorite skincare routine.

Words of Wisdom: "True beauty shines from the heart and dwells in the eyes." – Judith McNaught

From the Bible: "Charm may be false, and beauty may be fleeting, but the woman who fears Jehovah will be praised." —Proverbs 31:30

Reflection Question: What aspects of your outer beauty do you appreciate, and how can you celebrate them today?

May 24th: Finding Beauty in Nature

Nature is a constant reminder of the world's beauty. Today, focus on finding and celebrating the beauty in the natural world around you.

Spend time outdoors, observing the details of nature. Notice the colors of the flowers, the patterns of the leaves, the song of the birds, and the feel of the breeze. Let the beauty of nature fill you with awe and inspiration.

Celebrate nature's beauty by taking a walk in the park, tending to your garden, or simply sitting outside and soaking in the environment. Let nature's beauty remind you of the wonders of creation.

Words of Wisdom: "Just living is not enough... one must have sunshine, freedom, and a little flower." – Hans Christian Andersen

From the Bible: "The earth belongs to Jehovah, and so does everything in it, the productive land and those dwelling on it." —Psalm 24:1

Reflection Question: How can you find and celebrate the beauty of nature today, and what does it teach you about the world's wonder?

May 25th: Seeing Beauty in Others

Recognizing beauty in others helps us appreciate the diversity and uniqueness of everyone around us. Today, focus on seeing and celebrating the beauty in those you encounter.

Think about the people in your life and what makes them beautiful. It could be their kindness, their laughter, their wisdom, or their creativity. Acknowledge these qualities and let them inspire you.

Celebrate the beauty in others by expressing your appreciation. Compliment a friend, share your admiration with a loved one, or simply acknowledge someone's beauty silently in your heart.

Words of Wisdom: "When you love you radiate beauty, happiness, joy and every other good thing."— The Power by Rhonda Byrne

From the Bible: "And God went on to create the man in his image, in God's image he created him; male and female he created them." — Genesis 1:27

Reflection Question: What qualities make the people around you beautiful, and how can you celebrate their beauty today?

May 26th: Creating Beauty

Creating beauty through your actions and surroundings can bring joy and fulfillment. Today, focus on how you can contribute to the beauty in the world.

Think about ways you can add beauty to your environment or community. It could be through art, gardening, decorating your space, or acts of kindness. Recognize that creating beauty is an expression of your inner self.

Celebrate your ability to create beauty by engaging in a creative activity that you enjoy. Let your creativity flow and bring something beautiful into the world.

Words of Wisdom: "The creation of beauty is art." - Ralph Waldo Emerson

From the Bible: "Commit to Jehovah whatever you do, and he will establish your plans." —Proverbs 16:3

Reflection Question: How can you create beauty today, and what impact does this have on your life and the lives of others?

May 27th: Reflecting on Inner and Outer Beauty

Reflecting on the beauty within and around you helps deepen your appreciation for life's richness. Today, focus on integrating your reflections on inner and outer beauty.

Spend a quiet moment reflecting on the beauty you've discovered within yourself, in others, and in the world. Write down your thoughts and feelings, acknowledging the joy and inspiration these reflections bring.

Celebrate the culmination of your reflections by engaging in a gratitude practice. Give thanks for the beauty in your life and commit to recognizing and celebrating it every day.

Words of Wisdom: "Beauty is a radiance that originates from within and comes from inner security and strong character." - Jane Seymour

From the Bible: "Charm may be false, and beauty may be fleeting, but the woman who fears Jehovah will be praised." —Proverbs 31:30

Reflection Question: How have your reflections on beauty enriched your life, and how can you continue to celebrate beauty daily?

May 28th: Beauty in Everyday Moments

Beauty can be found in the simplest moments of daily life. Today, focus on recognizing and celebrating the beauty in your everyday experiences.

Pay attention to the small, beautiful moments throughout your day. It could be a warm smile from a stranger, the aroma of freshly brewed coffee, or the peacefulness of a quiet morning. Let these moments fill you with gratitude and joy.

Celebrate the beauty of everyday moments by being fully present and mindful. Appreciate the simple pleasures and the beauty they bring to your life.

Words of Wisdom: "Enjoy the little things in life, for one day you'll look back and realize they were the big things." – Kurt Vonnegut

From the Bible: "Come, let us sing joyfully to Jehovah! Let us shout in triumph to our Rock of salvation." —Psalm 95:1

Reflection Question: What beautiful moments can you find in your daily life today, and how can you celebrate these simple pleasures?

May 29th: Expressing Gratitude for Beauty

Expressing gratitude for the beauty in your life enhances your appreciation and joy. Today, focus on being grateful for the beauty you encounter.

Take time to notice and give thanks for the beauty in your surroundings, in yourself, and in others. Acknowledge the positive impact this beauty has on your well-being.

Celebrate your gratitude by sharing it with others. Express your appreciation for the beauty they bring into your life, and let them know how much it means to you.

Words of Wisdom: "The heart that gives thanks is a happy one, for we cannot feel thankful and unhappy at the same time." - Douglas Wood

From the Bible: "Praise Jah! Give thanks to Jehovah, for he is good; his loyal love endures forever." —Psalm 106:1

Reflection Question: How can you express gratitude for the beauty in your life today, and what positive effects does this gratitude have on you and others?

May 30th: Inspiring Others with Beauty

Sharing and inspiring others with the beauty you see and create can have a ripple effect. Today, focus on how you can inspire others to recognize and celebrate beauty.

Think about ways you can share your appreciation for beauty with others. It could be through your words, actions, or creative expressions. Inspire others to see the beauty in themselves and the world around them.

Celebrate your ability to inspire by sharing a beautiful experience or creation with someone today. Encourage them to find and celebrate their own beauty.

Words of Wisdom: "Your inner beauty is revealed through the power of your love" —The Power by Rhonda Byrne

From the Bible: "Likewise, let your light shine before men, so that they may see your fine works and give glory to your Father who is in the heavens." —Matthew 5:16

Reflection Question: How can you inspire others to recognize and celebrate beauty, and what impact can this have on their lives?

May 31st: Continuing the Celebration of Beauty

The celebration of beauty is an ongoing journey. Today, focus on continuing to recognize and celebrate beauty in all its forms every day.

Reflect on the beauty you've discovered this month and how it has enriched your life. Commit to making the recognition and celebration of beauty a daily practice.

Celebrate the ongoing journey by setting an intention to seek out and appreciate beauty in every moment. Let this practice bring you continuous joy, inspiration, and fulfillment.

Words of Wisdom: "You are the creator of your thoughts and your thoughts create your reality." —Dr Wayne Dyer

From the Bible: "Finally, brothers, whatever things are true, whatever things are of serious concern, whatever things are righteous, whatever things are chaste, whatever things are lovable, whatever things are well spoken of, whatever virtue there is and whatever praiseworthy thing there is, continue considering these things." —Philippians 4:8

Reflection Question: How can you continue to recognize and celebrate beauty every day, and what benefits does this practice bring to your life?

Chapter 3: Summer
Radiance and Self-Expression

Summer is a season of warmth, vitality, and radiance. It's a time when the world is alive with color, energy, and the fullness of life. Just as the sun shines its brightest, summer invites us to let our inner light shine and express our true selves with confidence and joy.

June is the beginning of summer, a time to embody self-confidence and express your inner strength. This month encourages you to reflect on your journey so far, recognizing the resilience and growth you've experienced. It's a time to express gratitude for the strengths you've developed and to honor the personal boundaries that protect your peace.

As the summer heat intensifies in July, so too does the opportunity to cultivate creativity and passion. This month invites you to harness your creative energy, exploring new avenues of self-expression and embracing the sensual pleasures of life. Whether it's through art, music, writing, or any other creative outlet, July is the perfect time to align with your purpose and passion. Celebrate your unique self-expression and let your creativity flow freely. In doing so, you not only nourish your soul but also contribute to the peace and beauty of the world around you.

August, the final month of summer, is a time for nourishing the soul and preparing for the transition into autumn. As the season begins to wind down, this is the perfect opportunity to bask in self-care rituals that replenish your energy and reconnect you with your inner wisdom. August encourages you to release self-limiting beliefs, making space for love and compassion to radiate from within.

In this chapter, as you journey through the summer months, you will explore how self-expression, creativity, and self-care can cultivate a deep sense of peace. Each devotion is designed to help you embrace your true self, find joy in the creative process, and nourish your soul, allowing you to radiate love and peace in all areas of your life.

June: Embodying Self-Confidence

Summer, with its bright and abundant light, invites us to embody self-confidence and radiate our true selves. This month, we focus on the themes of radiance and self-expression, harnessing the clarity and energy that summer brings. Just as the sun shines brilliantly, illuminating everything in its path, we too can shine with confidence and clarity.

Embodying self-confidence means recognizing our strengths, embracing our uniqueness, and expressing ourselves authentically. It's about standing tall in who we are and letting our inner light shine brightly. This month, we will explore ways to cultivate and celebrate our inner strength, set healthy boundaries, connect with our deepest desires, and radiate love and joy to those around us.

By tapping into the vibrant energy of summer, we can find the courage to express our true selves, fostering a sense of peace and fulfillment. Let's embark on this journey of self-confidence and self-expression, celebrating the radiant beings we are meant to be.

Week 1: Expressing Gratitude for Inner Strength

Gratitude is a powerful practice that can transform our perspective and enhance our inner strength. This week, we focus on expressing gratitude for the personal strengths and past achievements that have built our resilience and self-confidence. By recognizing and appreciating these qualities, we reinforce our ability to face challenges and embrace our true selves.

Each day, we will take time to reflect on different aspects of our inner strength, acknowledging the experiences and qualities that have shaped us. This practice not only boosts our confidence but also fosters a deep sense of peace and self-assurance. Let's celebrate our journey and the powerful women we have become.

June 1st: Recognizing Your Strengths

Start the week by recognizing the strengths that define you. Reflect on the qualities that have helped you navigate life's challenges—your determination, compassion, creativity, or resilience.

Think about specific instances where these strengths have guided you through difficult times. Acknowledge the role they played in your achievements and personal growth.

Express gratitude for these strengths. Take a moment to say thank you to yourself for being strong, capable, and resilient. Embrace these qualities as integral parts of who you are.

Words of Wisdom: "Compassion for others begins with kindness to ourselves." —Pema Chodron

From the Bible: "But the fruitage of the spirit is love, joy, peace, patience, kindness, goodness, faith." —Galatians 5:22

Reflection Question: What personal strengths have helped you overcome challenges, and how can you express gratitude for them today?

June 2nd: Celebrating Past Achievements

Today, focus on celebrating your past achievements. Reflect on the milestones you've reached, both big and small, and the effort it took to get there.

Identify a specific achievement that you're proud of. Consider the skills, perseverance, and dedication it required. Acknowledge the hard work and resilience you demonstrated.

Express gratitude for your accomplishments. Celebrate your success and recognize it as a testament to your inner strength and capability.

Words of Wisdom: "When you connect to the silence within you, that is when you can make sense of the disturbance going on around you." —Dr. Joe Dispenza

From the Bible: "When words are many, transgression is unavoidable, but whoever restrains his lips is prudent." —Proverbs 10:19

Reflection Question: What past achievement are you most proud of, and how can you celebrate this accomplishment today?

June 3rd: Embracing Resilience

Resilience is the ability to bounce back from adversity. Today, focus on the moments when you've shown resilience and the strength it took to overcome obstacles.

Think about a time when you faced a significant challenge and emerged stronger. Reflect on the inner strength and determination that carried you through.

Express gratitude for your resilience. Appreciate the ability to endure, adapt, and grow from difficult experiences. Recognize that each challenge has made you stronger and more capable.

Words of Wisdom: "What lies before us and what lies behind us are small matters compared to what lies within us." —Michael Singer

From the Bible: "Happy is the man who keeps on enduring trial, because on becoming approved he will receive the crown of life that Jehovah promised to those who continue loving Him." —James 1:12

Reflection Question: How has resilience shaped you, and what challenges have you overcome that you can be grateful for today?

June 4th: Gratitude for Growth

Growth often comes from facing and overcoming challenges. Today, focus on expressing gratitude for the personal growth you've experienced through difficult times.

Reflect on a period of your life where you experienced significant growth. Consider the lessons learned, the skills developed, and the person you've become as a result.

Express gratitude for this growth. Acknowledge the journey and the strength it took to evolve. Celebrate the progress you've made and the resilience you've shown.

Words of Wisdom: "The key to growth is the introduction of higher dimensions of consciousness into our awareness." —Lynne McTaggart

From the Bible: "But grow in the undeserved kindness and knowledge of our Lord and Savior Jesus Christ." —2 Peter 3:18

Reflection Question: What period of growth are you grateful for, and how has it shaped who you are today?

June 5th: Thanking Your Support System

Recognizing the support from others is crucial in understanding our own strength. Today, express gratitude for the people who have supported you and contributed to your resilience.

Think about the individuals who have been there for you during tough times—family, friends, mentors, or colleagues. Reflect on how their support has helped you overcome challenges and grow stronger.

Express gratitude for these relationships. Reach out to someone who has supported you and thank them for their presence and encouragement.

Words of Wisdom: "In the midst of movement and chaos, keep stillness inside of you." —Deepak Chopra

From the Bible: "Two are better than one, because they have a good reward for their hard work." —Ecclesiastes 4:9

Reflection Question: Who has supported you in your journey, and how can you express gratitude for their support today?

June 6th: Appreciating Self-Compassion

Self-compassion is a key aspect of inner strength. Today, focus on appreciating your ability to be kind to yourself, especially during challenging times.

Reflect on moments when you've practiced self-compassion. Consider how being gentle and understanding with yourself has helped you navigate difficulties and maintain your well-being.

Express gratitude for your self-compassion. Acknowledge the importance of treating yourself with the same kindness and care that you offer to others.

Words of Wisdom: "Love yourself enough to create an environment in your life that is conducive to the nourishment of your personal growth." —Michael Singer

From the Bible: "By this all will know that you are my disciples—if you have love among yourselves." —John 13:35

Reflection Question: How has self-compassion helped you through difficult times, and how can you appreciate this quality in yourself today?

June 7th: Honoring Personal Growth

End the week by honoring your personal growth and the journey you've undertaken. Reflect on the cumulative experiences that have contributed to your inner strength and confidence.

Consider the growth you've experienced over the years. Reflect on the challenges faced, the achievements celebrated, and the lessons learned. Recognize the strong, capable person you've become.

Express gratitude for your journey. Celebrate your growth and honor the strength it has taken to get where you are today.

Words of Wisdom: "When you are grateful, fear disappears, and abundance appears." —Rhonda Byrne

From the Bible: "Jehovah himself will bless his people with peace." —Psalm 29:11

Reflection Question: How can you honor and celebrate your personal growth today, recognizing the journey that has brought you here?

Week 2: Honoring Personal Boundaries

Setting and respecting personal boundaries is essential for healthy self-expression and maintaining positive relationships. Boundaries help protect our emotional well-being, define our values, and ensure that we honor our own needs and limits. This week, we focus on the importance of personal boundaries, how to establish them, and how they contribute to our overall peace and confidence.

By honoring our boundaries, we communicate our needs clearly and respectfully to others. This practice not only enhances our self-respect but also fosters mutual respect in our relationships. Each day's devotion will guide you in exploring different aspects of personal boundaries, helping you create and uphold boundaries that support your well-being and inspire your self-expression.

June 8th: Understanding Personal Boundaries

Personal boundaries are the limits we set to protect our emotional and physical well-being. Today, focus on understanding what personal boundaries are and why they are important.

Reflect on areas of your life where you feel stretched too thin or taken for granted. Consider how setting clear boundaries could improve your emotional health and relationships.

Think about one boundary you need to set for your well-being. Commit to clearly communicating this boundary to those it affects, and honor it as an act of self-respect.

Words of Wisdom: "Boundaries are not a rejection of others but a statement of what you stand for." —Sadhguru

From the Bible: "Above all the things that you guard, safeguard your heart, for out of it are the sources of life." —Proverbs 4:23

Reflection Question: What boundary do you need to set to protect your emotional well-being, and how will you communicate and honor it?

June 9th: Identifying Your Limits

Recognizing your limits is crucial for setting effective boundaries. Today, focus on identifying the areas in your life where you need to establish or reinforce boundaries.

Reflect on situations where you feel overwhelmed or stressed. Consider whether these feelings stem from overextending yourself or allowing others to overstep your boundaries.

Choose one specific area where you need to set a clearer limit. Decide what action you will take to establish this boundary and protect your well-being.

Words of Wisdom: "The more you make your thoughts and beliefs more powerful than your fears, the less your fears will control you." — Dr. Joe Dispenza

From the Bible: "Just let your word 'Yes' mean Yes, and your 'No,' No." —Matthew 5:37

Reflection Question: Where do you need to set clearer limits in your life, and what steps will you take to enforce this boundary?

June 10th: Communicating Boundaries Respectfully

Clear communication is key to setting and maintaining boundaries. Today, focus on how to communicate your boundaries respectfully and assertively.

Think about a boundary you need to communicate. Plan how you will express this boundary clearly and respectfully to those involved. Use "I" statements to convey your needs without blaming or criticizing others.

Practice this communication today. Speak with confidence and kindness, ensuring that your message is understood and respected.

Words of Wisdom: "When you argue with reality, you lose, but only 100% of the time." —Byron Katie

From the Bible: "Let a rotten word not come out of your mouth, but only what is good for building up." —Ephesians 4:29

Reflection Question: How can you communicate your boundaries clearly and respectfully, ensuring they are understood and honored?

June 11th: Respecting Others' Boundaries

Honoring personal boundaries also involves respecting the boundaries of others. Today, focus on being mindful and respectful of the limits set by those around you.

Reflect on your interactions with others. Are there areas where you might be overstepping their boundaries? Consider how you can show respect and support for their limits.

Practice respecting others' boundaries by asking for their preferences and needs. Show empathy and understanding, recognizing that mutual respect strengthens relationships.

Words of Wisdom: "A boundary is not something you create; it's something you live by." —Sadhguru

From the Bible: "Look out not only for your own interests, but also for the interests of others." —Philippians 2:4

Reflection Question: How can you be more mindful of others' boundaries, and what actions will you take to respect and support their limits?

June 12th: Reinforcing Boundaries

Reinforcing boundaries is essential to ensure they are respected. Today, focus on ways to consistently uphold and reinforce your personal boundaries.

Reflect on a boundary you have set. Consider any challenges you've faced in maintaining it. Think about strategies to reinforce this boundary consistently, even when it's difficult.

Practice reinforcing your boundary today. Be firm and clear, yet kind, when reminding others of your limits. Remember that reinforcing boundaries is an ongoing process that requires persistence and self-respect.

Words of Wisdom: "When you say yes to others, make sure you are not saying no to yourself." —Paulo Coelho

From the Bible: "Like a city that has been breached and left without a wall is the man who cannot control his temper." —Proverbs 25:28

Reflection Question: How can you consistently reinforce a personal boundary, and what strategies will help you maintain it effectively?

June 13th: Balancing Flexibility and Firmness

Finding a balance between flexibility and firmness in setting boundaries is important. Today, focus on maintaining this balance to ensure your boundaries are effective and adaptable.

Think about a boundary that requires flexibility. Reflect on how you can be firm in upholding it while also being adaptable to changing circumstances.

Practice balancing flexibility and firmness today. Be open to adjusting your boundaries, when necessary, but remain firm in protecting your core needs and values.

Words of Wisdom: "Flexibility in life is a sign of life; rigidity, a sign of death." —Sadhguru

From the Bible: "Let your reasonableness become known to all men." —Philippians 4:5

Reflection Question: How can you balance flexibility and firmness in maintaining your boundaries, ensuring they are both adaptable and protective?

June 14th: Celebrating Boundary Successes

Celebrate your successes in setting and maintaining boundaries. Today, focus on acknowledging and appreciating the positive impact boundaries have had on your life.

Reflect on a boundary you've successfully set and maintained. Consider how it has improved your emotional well-being and relationships. Take a moment to appreciate your effort and commitment.

Celebrate this success by doing something special for yourself. Recognize that honoring your boundaries is an act of self-love and respect, and it deserves to be celebrated.

Words of Wisdom: "The power for creating a better future is contained in the present moment." —Eckhart Tolle

From the Bible: "The measuring lines have fallen for me in pleasant places. Indeed, my inheritance is beautiful." —Psalm 16:6

Reflection Question: What boundary success can you celebrate today, and how has it positively impacted your well-being and relationships?

Week 3: Connecting with the Heart's Desires

Understanding and connecting with your heart's desires is essential for living a fulfilled and joyful life. This week, we focus on exploring our deepest aspirations and dreams. By taking the time to reflect on what truly brings us joy, we can align our actions with our passions and create a life that resonates with our innermost desires. This week's devotions will guide you in uncovering your true aspirations, encouraging you to pursue what brings you the greatest fulfillment and happiness.

June 15th: Listening to Your Heart

Your heart often knows what truly brings you joy and fulfillment. Today, focus on listening to your heart to understand your deepest desires.

Spend some quiet time in reflection. Think about moments when you felt genuinely happy and fulfilled. What activities, people, or environments were involved? What passions or dreams were you pursuing?

Write down these insights and consider how you can incorporate more of these elements into your life. Trust that your heart's desires are a guide to your true purpose and joy.

Words of Wisdom: "The heart knows what it wants, and it often shows us through feelings of joy and fulfillment." —Pema Chodron

From the Bible: "In all your ways take notice of him, and he will make your paths straight." —Proverbs 3:6

Reflection Question: What moments of joy and fulfillment can you recall, and how can you listen to your heart's desires today?

June 16th: Identifying Your Passions

Passions are the activities and pursuits that ignite your spirit. Today, focus on identifying what you are truly passionate about.

Think about what activities make you lose track of time because you are so engaged and happy. Reflect on hobbies, interests, or work that excite and inspire you.

Write down these passions and consider how you can make more time for them in your life. Embrace your passions as a source of joy and fulfillment.

Words of Wisdom: "Passion is energy. Feel the power that comes from focusing on what excites you." —Oprah Winfrey

From the Bible: "Be industrious, not lazy. Be aglow with the spirit." —Romans 12:11

Reflection Question: What are you truly passionate about, and how can you incorporate these passions into your daily life?

June 17th: Pursuing Your Dreams

Dreams give our lives direction and purpose. Today, focus on pursuing your dreams with determination and confidence.

Reflect on your biggest dreams and aspirations. What goals have you set for yourself? What steps can you take to move closer to achieving these dreams?

Commit to taking one small action today that brings you closer to your dream. Remember that every step, no matter how small, is progress toward a fulfilling and joyful life.

Words of Wisdom: "The more you focus on what you want, the closer you move toward it." —Rhonda Byrne

From the Bible: "For I know the thoughts that I am thinking toward you, thoughts of peace, and not of calamity, to give you a future and a hope." —Jeremiah 29:11

Reflection Question: What are your biggest dreams, and what small step can you take today to pursue them?

June 18th: Embracing Your Unique Gifts

Everyone has unique gifts and talents that contribute to their purpose and joy. Today, focus on embracing and utilizing your unique gifts.

Think about the skills and talents that come naturally to you. How have you used these gifts in the past, and how can they bring joy and fulfillment to your life?

Celebrate your unique abilities by finding ways to use them more often. Embrace your gifts as part of your identity and path to joy.

Words of Wisdom: "Your gifts are not for you alone. They are for the world to see and benefit from." —Sadhguru

From the Bible: "Just as each one has received a gift, use it in ministering to one another." —1 Peter 4:10

Reflection Question: What unique gifts do you possess, and how can you use them to bring joy and fulfillment to your life?

June 19th: Aligning with Your Values

Living in alignment with your values brings a deep sense of peace and fulfillment. Today, focus on understanding and aligning your life with your core values.

Reflect on what values are most important to you—honesty, kindness, integrity, or creativity, for example. Consider how these values guide your actions and decisions.

Commit to making choices that align with your values. Recognize that living according to your values leads to a more authentic and fulfilling life.

Words of Wisdom: "To live in alignment with your values is to create peace within your soul." —Michael Singer

From the Bible: "To do righteousness and justice is more desirable to Jehovah than sacrifice." —Proverbs 21:3

Reflection Question: What core values guide your life, and how can you align your actions with these values today?

June 20th: Visualizing Your Ideal Life

Visualization is a powerful tool for achieving your desires. Today, focus on visualizing your ideal life in vivid detail.

Find a quiet place and close your eyes. Imagine your ideal life in five or ten years. What are you doing? Who is with you? How do you feel?

Write down your vision and consider what steps you can take to make this vision a reality. Let this visualization inspire and motivate you to pursue your heart's desires.

Words of Wisdom: "See the things you want as already yours." — Rhonda Byrne

From the Bible: "Write down the vision, and inscribe it clearly on tablets, so that the one reading aloud may do so easily." —Habakkuk 2:2

Reflection Question: What does your ideal life look like, and what steps can you take to move toward this vision?

June 21st: Taking Inspired Action

Dreams and desires require action to become reality. Today, focus on taking inspired action to pursue what brings you joy and fulfillment.

Reflect on the desires and goals you've identified this week. What actions can you take to move closer to achieving them?

Commit to taking one inspired action today. Whether it's researching a new opportunity, starting a project, or reaching out for support, take a step forward with confidence and determination.

Words of Wisdom: "The power of the mind is an incredible thing. What you think, you become." —Dr. Joe Dispenza

From the Bible: "Commit to Jehovah whatever you do, and your plans will succeed." —Proverbs 16:3

Reflection Question: What inspired action can you take today to pursue your heart's desires, and how will this step bring you closer to fulfillment?

Week 4: Radiating Love and Joy

Radiating love and joy to those around us creates a ripple effect that enhances not only their lives but also our own. This week, we focus on spreading positivity and kindness, recognizing that these acts enrich our sense of peace and happiness. By sharing love and joy, we cultivate a supportive and uplifting environment, fostering deeper connections and a more fulfilling life. Each day's devotion will guide you in exploring ways to radiate love and joy, helping you to make a positive impact on the world around you.

June 22nd: Sharing Kind Words

Words have the power to uplift and inspire. Today, focus on sharing kind words with those around you.

Take a moment to express appreciation or encouragement to someone in your life. Whether it's a friend, family member, or colleague, let them know how much they mean to you.

Notice the positive impact your words have on others. Recognize that by spreading kindness, you enhance your own sense of joy and connection.

Words of Wisdom: "Kindness is the language which the deaf can hear and the blind can see." —Mark Twain

From the Bible: "Pleasant sayings are a honeycomb, sweet to the soul and a healing to the bones." —Proverbs 16:24

Reflection Question: How can you use your words to uplift and inspire someone today?

June 23rd: Acts of Kindness

Simple acts of kindness can transform someone's day. Today, focus on performing small acts of kindness for others.

Think of a way you can brighten someone's day—buy a coffee for a stranger, help a neighbor, or send a thoughtful message. These small gestures have a big impact.

Reflect on how these acts of kindness make you feel. Notice the joy and fulfillment that come from spreading positivity.

Words of Wisdom: "Remember there's no such thing as a small act of kindness. Every act creates a ripple." —Scott Adams

From the Bible: "Do not forget to do good and to share with others, for with such sacrifices God is well pleased." —Hebrews 13:16

Reflection Question: What small act of kindness can you perform today, and how does it enhance your own sense of joy?

June 24th: Listening with Love

Listening is a powerful way to show love and support. Today, focus on being a compassionate and attentive listener.

When someone speaks to you, give them your full attention. Listen without interrupting or offering unsolicited advice. Simply be present and empathetic.

Notice how this deep listening strengthens your connection with others. Recognize that offering your attention is a valuable act of love.

Words of Wisdom: "True beauty is the radiance of your spirit shining outward, a reflection of your inner essence." —Sadhguru, *Inner Engineering*

From the Bible: "She is clothed with strength and splendor, and she looks to the future with confidence." —Proverbs 31:25

Reflection Question: How can you use fashion to express your individuality today, and what impact does this have on your confidence and self-perception?

June 25th: Spreading Joy Through Service

Serving others is a meaningful way to spread joy. Today, focus on finding a way to serve someone in your community.

Look for opportunities to volunteer or help someone in need. Whether it's through a local charity, community project, or helping a neighbor, your service can make a difference.

Reflect on the fulfillment you feel from serving others. Recognize that acts of service not only benefit those you help but also enrich your own life with purpose and joy.

Words of Wisdom: "The more we give, the more we receive. The more we care, the more the world changes." —Michael Singer

From the Bible: "Just as each one has received a gift, use it in ministering to one another." —1 Peter 4:10

Reflection Question: How can you serve someone in your community today, and what joy does this act of service bring to you?

June 26th: Creating Joyful Spaces

Your environment can influence your mood and well-being. Today, focus on creating spaces that radiate joy and positivity.

Take time to declutter and brighten your living or work space. Add elements that make you happy, such as plants, photos, or inspirational quotes.

Notice how a joyful environment affects your mood and productivity. Recognize that creating a positive space is an act of self-love that enhances your daily life.

Words of Wisdom: "Your space is a reflection of your mind. Clear it, and you clear your thoughts." —Sadhguru

From the Bible: "For as he thinks in his heart, so he is." —Proverbs 23:7

Reflection Question: How can you create a joyful and positive environment today, and what impact does this have on your well-being?

June 27th: Spreading Positivity Online

Social media and online interactions offer opportunities to spread positivity. Today, focus on using your online presence to share love and joy.

Post something uplifting on your social media accounts—a positive quote, a beautiful photo, or an encouraging message. Engage with others positively and supportively.

Reflect on the impact of your positive online interactions. Recognize that spreading joy in the digital world can reach and uplift many people.

Words of Wisdom: "What you focus on expands. Spread positivity and watch your world transform." —Wayne Dyer

From the Bible: "Speak truth each one of you with his neighbor, because we are members belonging to one another." —Ephesians 4:25

Reflection Question: How can you use your online presence to spread positivity today, and what difference does it make?

June 28th: Celebrating Shared Joy

Joy multiplies when shared with others. Today, focus on celebrating moments of joy with the people around you.

Plan a small gathering, a phone call, or an outing with loved ones. Share laughter, stories, and positive experiences. Celebrate the connections that bring joy into your life.

Reflect on the shared joy and the bonds it strengthens. Recognize that celebrating together enhances your own happiness and fosters a sense of community.

Words of Wisdom: "Joy increases as you give it, and diminishes as you try to keep it for yourself." —Michael Singer

From the Bible: "Rejoice with those who rejoice; weep with those who weep." —Romans 12:15

Reflection Question: How can you share and celebrate moments of joy with others today, and how does this deepen your connections?

June 29th: Practicing Loving-Kindness Meditation

Loving-kindness meditation is a powerful way to cultivate compassion and radiate love. Today, focus on practicing this form of meditation to spread joy and positivity.

Find a quiet place to sit comfortably. Close your eyes and take a few deep breaths. Begin by silently repeating phrases like "May I be happy, may I be healthy, may I be safe, may I live with ease." Gradually extend these wishes to others—first to loved ones, then to acquaintances, and finally to all beings.

Notice how this meditation fills you with a sense of love and peace. Recognize that sending out loving-kindness not only benefits others but also enhances your own well-being.

Words of Wisdom: "Love and kindness are never wasted. They always make a difference." —Helen James

From the Bible: "This is my commandment, that you love one another just as I have loved you." —John 15:12

Reflection Question: How does practicing loving-kindness meditation make you feel, and how can you incorporate this practice into your daily life?

June 30th: Gratitude for Love and Joy

End the week by expressing gratitude for the love and joy in your life. Today, focus on acknowledging and appreciating the positive emotions and connections you've cultivated.

Reflect on the moments of love and joy you've experienced recently. Consider the people, experiences, and practices that have brought these feelings into your life.

Write down three things you are grateful for regarding love and joy. Celebrate these blessings and commit to nurturing them in the future.

Words of Wisdom: "Gratitude is the memory of the heart." —Jean Baptiste Massieu

From the Bible: "Give thanks to Jehovah, for he is good; his loyal love endures forever." —Psalm 136:1

Reflection Question: What moments of love and joy are you grateful for, and how can you continue to cultivate these feelings in your life?

July: Cultivating Creativity and Passion

Summer is a season of vibrant energy and long, sun-filled days, making it the perfect time to cultivate creativity and passion. This month, we explore how engaging in creative activities and pursuing our passions can enrich our lives and bring joy. Whether it's starting a new hobby, rekindling an old interest, or simply allowing ourselves to dream and create, summer offers an abundance of opportunities to ignite our inner fire.

Creativity and passion are essential for a fulfilling life. They allow us to express our true selves, connect with others on a deeper level, and find meaning and purpose. This month, we will delve into various ways to harness our creative energy, embrace life's pleasures, and align our actions with our deepest passions. Let the warmth and light of summer inspire you to explore new interests and reignite the passions that make your heart sing.

Week 1: Harnessing Creative Energy

Harnessing creative energy allows us to express our true selves and find joy in the process of creation. This week, we focus on tapping into our creativity, exploring various ways to channel our energies into meaningful and fulfilling activities. Whether it's through arts, writing, music, or other expressive outlets, creativity helps us connect with our inner passions and share our unique gifts with the world. Each day's devotion will offer ideas and encouragement to inspire your creative pursuits, helping you discover the joy and fulfillment that comes from embracing your creative spirit.

July 1st: Exploring New Artistic Mediums

Engaging with new artistic mediums can spark your creativity. Today, focus on exploring a new form of art—painting, sculpting, or photography.

Choose an artistic activity you've always wanted to try. Gather the necessary materials and set aside time to immerse yourself in the creative process. Don't worry about the outcome; enjoy the act of creation.

Notice how trying something new stimulates your mind and spirit. Embrace the freedom to experiment and discover new aspects of your creative self.

Words of Wisdom: "The creative mind plays with the objects it loves." —Carl Jung

From the Bible: "And I have filled him with the spirit of God, in wisdom, and in understanding, and in knowledge, and in all kinds of craftsmanship." —Exodus 31:3

Reflection Question: What new artistic medium can you explore today, and how does it feel to engage in this creative activity?

July 2nd: Writing from the Heart

Writing is a powerful way to express your thoughts and feelings. Today, focus on writing from the heart, whether through journaling, poetry, or storytelling.

Find a quiet space and allow your thoughts to flow onto the paper. Write about your dreams, experiences, or emotions without censoring yourself. Let your writing be an authentic reflection of your inner world.

Notice how writing helps you process your thoughts and connect with your true self. Embrace the clarity and relief that comes from expressing yourself through words.

Words of Wisdom: "When you write, you lay out a line of words. The line of words is a miner's pick, a woodcarver's gouge, a surgeon's probe." —Annie Dillard

From the Bible: "My heart is stirred by a good theme as I recite my verses for the king; my tongue is the stylus of a skilled copyist." —Psalm 45:1

Reflection Question: How does writing from the heart help you express your true self, and what insights do you gain from this practice?

July 3rd: Making Music

Music has the power to uplift and inspire. Today, focus on making music, whether by playing an instrument, singing, or composing.

Choose a musical activity that resonates with you. Spend time creating or enjoying music, allowing yourself to be fully immersed in the experience. Let the melodies and rhythms inspire you.

Notice the joy and energy that music brings into your life. Embrace the way it connects you to your emotions and enhances your creative expression.

Words of Wisdom: "Music is the divine way to tell beautiful, poetic things to the heart." —Pablo Casals

From the Bible: "Sing to Jehovah a new song; Sing to Jehovah, all the earth." —Psalm 96:1

Reflection Question: How does making music inspire and uplift you, and what creative energy do you feel from this experience?

July 4th: Creating with Nature

Nature is a profound source of inspiration. Today, focus on creating art using natural materials like leaves, flowers, rocks, or sand.

Take a walk outside and gather materials that catch your eye. Use these natural elements to create a piece of art, whether it's a simple arrangement or a more intricate design.

Notice the connection between nature and your creativity. Embrace the beauty and simplicity of creating with the earth's offerings.

Words of Wisdom: "In every walk with nature, one receives far more than he seeks." —John Muir

From the Bible: "The earth is Jehovah's, and everything in it, the productive land and those dwelling on it." —Psalm 24:1

Reflection Question: How does creating with natural materials enhance your connection to nature and your creative process?

July 5th: Crafting and DIY Projects

Crafting and DIY projects can be fun and rewarding. Today, focus on engaging in a crafting activity that brings you joy.

Choose a craft project that excites you, whether it's knitting, woodworking, or making jewelry. Gather your materials and spend time bringing your project to life.

Notice the satisfaction and pride you feel in creating something with your hands. Embrace the creativity and patience that crafting requires.

Words of Wisdom: "The creative process is a process of surrender, not control." —Julia Cameron

From the Bible: "But now, O Jehovah, you are our Father. We are the clay, and you are our Potter; We are all the work of your hand." —Isaiah 64:8

Reflection Question: What crafting project can you start today, and how does it feel to create something with your hands?

July 6th: Exploring Creative Writing

Creative writing allows you to explore new worlds and ideas. Today, focus on writing a short story, poem, or play that reflects your imagination.

Let your mind wander and create a narrative that excites you. Don't worry about perfection; focus on the joy of storytelling and the creative process.

Notice how creative writing helps you explore new perspectives and ideas. Embrace the freedom and excitement that comes from creating your own literary work.

Words of Wisdom: "There is no greater agony than bearing an untold story inside you." —Maya Angelou

From the Bible: "Write down the vision, and inscribe it clearly on tablets, so that the one reading aloud from it may do so easily." — Habakkuk 2:2

Reflection Question: How does creative writing allow you to explore your imagination, and what stories or ideas can you bring to life today?

July 7th: Dancing with Joy

Dance is a joyful expression of movement and rhythm. Today, focus on dancing freely to your favorite music, letting your body move to the beat.

Find a space where you can dance without inhibition. Choose music that makes you feel alive and happy, and let your body move naturally to the rhythm.

Notice the freedom and joy that dancing brings. Embrace the way it connects you to your emotions and enhances your creative expression.

Words of Wisdom: "To watch us dance is to hear our hearts speak." — Hopi Proverb

From the Bible: "Praise his name with dancing; Play the tambourine and the harp to him." —Psalm 149:3

Reflection Question: How does dancing make you feel, and what creative energy do you experience through movement and rhythm?

Week 2: Embracing Sensuality and Pleasure

Embracing life's pleasures involves connecting deeply with our senses and finding joy in the physical world around us. This week, we focus on appreciating the simple pleasures that engage our senses—sight, sound, taste, touch, and smell. By being fully present and mindful of these experiences, we can enhance our sense of joy and fulfillment. Drawing from the wisdom of various spiritual and philosophical teachings, each day's devotion will guide you in celebrating the beauty and delight found in everyday moments.

July 8th: Delighting in Visual Beauty

The world is filled with visual wonders that can bring us joy and inspiration. Today, focus on appreciating the beauty you see around you.

Take a walk in nature, visit an art gallery, or simply sit in a park. Observe the colors, shapes, and details of your surroundings. Allow yourself to be fully present and appreciative of the visual beauty you encounter.

Notice how these sights uplift your spirit and bring a sense of peace and joy. Embrace the power of visual beauty as a source of inspiration and delight.

Words of Wisdom: "The soul that sees beauty may sometimes walk alone." —Johann Wolfgang von Goethe

From the Bible: "The heavens are declaring the glory of God; The skies proclaim the work of his hands." —Psalm 19:1

Reflection Question: How can you take time today to appreciate the visual beauty around you, and what impact does it have on your mood and spirit?

July 9th: Savoring the Sounds of Life

Sound has the ability to move us deeply and bring immense pleasure. Today, focus on savoring the sounds that surround you.

Listen to your favorite music, the sounds of nature, or the laughter of loved ones. Be mindful of how these sounds make you feel and allow yourself to be fully immersed in the auditory experience.

Notice how sound can elevate your mood and create a sense of connection and joy. Embrace the auditory pleasures that enhance your daily life.

Words of Wisdom: "The earth has music for those who listen." — George Santayana

From the Bible: "Let everything that has breath praise Jah. Praise Jah!" —Psalm 150:6

Reflection Question: What sounds bring you joy, and how can you incorporate more of these auditory pleasures into your day?

July 10th: Tasting Life's Flavors

The sense of taste allows us to savor the richness of life's flavors. Today, focus on enjoying the taste of the foods and drinks you consume.

Choose a meal or snack that you particularly enjoy. Eat slowly and mindfully, paying attention to the flavors, textures, and aromas. Let yourself fully experience and appreciate each bite.

Notice how mindful eating enhances your enjoyment and satisfaction. Embrace the pleasure of tasting and savoring the foods that bring you joy.

Words of Wisdom: "The discovery of a new dish does more for human happiness than the discovery of a new star." —Jean Anthelme Brillat-Savarin

From the Bible: "Taste and see that Jehovah is good; Happy is the man who takes refuge in him." —Psalm 34:8

Reflection Question: How can you practice mindful eating today, and what foods bring you the most joy and pleasure?

July 11th: Feeling the Touch of Life

Touch connects us deeply with the physical world and brings comfort and joy. Today, focus on appreciating the sense of touch in your daily experiences.

Spend time engaging in activities that involve touch—petting an animal, hugging a loved one, or feeling the textures of different materials. Be mindful of the sensations and how they make you feel.

Notice how touch enhances your sense of connection and well-being. Embrace the pleasure of tactile experiences that bring you comfort and joy.

Words of Wisdom: "Sometimes the most ordinary things could be made extraordinary, simply by doing them with the right people." — Elizabeth Green

From the Bible: "A soothing tongue is a tree of life, but a deceitful tongue crushes the spirit." —Proverbs 15:4

Reflection Question: How can you be more mindful of the sense of touch today, and what tactile experiences bring you the most joy?

July 12th: Savoring Aromas

The sense of smell can evoke powerful memories and emotions. Today, focus on savoring the aromas around you and appreciating their impact on your mood and well-being.

Choose a scent that you love—fresh flowers, a favorite perfume, or the smell of baked goods. Take time to inhale deeply and savor the aroma, noticing how it makes you feel.

Notice how certain scents can uplift your spirit and create a sense of joy and nostalgia. Embrace the pleasure of savoring delightful aromas.

Words of Wisdom: "The sense of smell can transport you instantly across time and space." —Helen Keller

From the Bible: "May my prayer be as incense prepared before you, my uplifted hands like the evening grain offering." —Psalm 141:2

Reflection Question: What aromas bring you joy, and how can you incorporate more of these scents into your daily life?

July 13th: Embracing Life's Simple Pleasures

Life's simple pleasures often bring the greatest joy. Today, focus on appreciating and embracing these small moments of happiness.

Think about the simple pleasures that bring you joy—reading a book, sipping tea, or watching the sunset. Make time to indulge in these activities, being fully present and appreciative.

Notice how these simple pleasures enhance your well-being and create a sense of contentment. Embrace the joy found in life's everyday moments.

Words of Wisdom: "Simplicity is the ultimate sophistication." — Leonardo da Vinci

From the Bible: "Better is a little with the fear of Jehovah than great wealth along with anxiety." —Proverbs 15:16

Reflection Question: What simple pleasures bring you the most joy, and how can you make more time for them in your daily life?

July 14th: Connecting with the Present Moment

Being fully present enhances our appreciation of life's pleasures. Today, focus on connecting with the present moment and finding joy in the here and now.

Practice mindfulness by paying attention to your senses. Notice what you see, hear, taste, touch, and smell in each moment. Allow yourself to be fully immersed in the present experience.

Notice how being present enhances your sense of joy and peace. Embrace the beauty and pleasure found in the present moment.

Words of Wisdom: "Life is a succession of moments. To live each one is to succeed." —Corita Kent

From the Bible: "So, never be anxious about the next day, for the next day will have its own anxieties. Each day has enough of its own troubles." —Matthew 6:34

Reflection Question: How can you practice being fully present today, and what joys can you find in the present moment?

Week 3: Aligning with Purpose and Passion

Living a life aligned with purpose and passion brings deep fulfillment and joy. This week, we focus on reflecting on our life's purpose and understanding how to align our daily actions with our deeper passions. By exploring what truly matters to us and making conscious choices that reflect our values and desires, we can create a life that resonates with our true selves. Each day's devotion will guide you in uncovering your purpose, nurturing your passions, and taking steps toward a more intentional and fulfilling life.

July 15th: Discovering Your Life's Purpose

Understanding your life's purpose begins with introspection. Today, focus on reflecting on what truly matters to you and what you feel called to do.

Spend time in quiet reflection or journaling. Ask yourself questions like: What activities make me feel most alive? What do I deeply care about? How do I want to contribute to the world?

Write down your thoughts and look for common themes. Recognize that discovering your purpose is a journey and may evolve over time.

Words of Wisdom: "Your purpose in life is to find your purpose and give your whole heart and soul to it." —Gautama Buddha

From the Bible: "For this very reason, put forth all earnest effort to supply to your faith goodness, to your goodness knowledge." —2 Peter 1:5

Reflection Question: What activities and values make you feel most alive, and how do they point toward your life's purpose?

July 16th: Aligning Daily Actions with Your Purpose

Once you understand your purpose, the next step is to align your daily actions with it. Today, focus on integrating your purpose into your everyday life.

Identify one area of your life where you can make a small change to reflect your purpose. It could be in your work, relationships, or personal habits. Set a specific goal to act in alignment with your purpose.

Take this step today and observe how it makes you feel. Notice the sense of fulfillment that comes from living authentically and purposefully.

Words of Wisdom: "Don't aim at success. The more you aim at it and make it a target, the more you are going to miss it. For success, like happiness, cannot be pursued; it must ensue." —Viktor Frankl

From the Bible: "The steps of a man are established by Jehovah; He finds delight in his way." —Psalm 37:23

Reflection Question: What small change can you make today to align your actions with your purpose, and how does this shift impact your sense of fulfillment?

July 17th: Nurturing Your Passions

Passions are the fuel that drive your purpose. Today, focus on identifying and nurturing the passions that bring you joy and energy.

Reflect on the activities and interests that ignite your enthusiasm. How can you make more time for these passions in your daily life?

Choose one passion to focus on today. Dedicate time to it and fully immerse yourself in the experience. Notice how this nourishes your spirit and aligns with your purpose.

Words of Wisdom: "Passion is the genesis of genius." —Tony Robbins

From the Bible: "Whatever you do, work at it with all your heart, as for Jehovah and not for men." —Colossians 3:23

Reflection Question: What passion can you nurture today, and how does dedicating time to this passion align with your purpose?

July 18th: Overcoming Obstacles

Living a life aligned with purpose and passion often involves overcoming obstacles. Today, focus on identifying and addressing the challenges that hinder you from pursuing your purpose.

Think about the barriers that stand in your way. Are they external circumstances, internal fears, or limiting beliefs? Write them down and consider practical steps you can take to overcome them.

Take action on one step today. Remember that overcoming obstacles is a part of the journey and builds resilience and strength.

Words of Wisdom: "The brick walls are there for a reason. The brick walls are not there to keep us out. The brick walls are there to give us a chance to show how badly we want something." —Randy Pausch

From the Bible: "But those hoping in Jehovah will regain power; they will soar on wings like eagles. They will run and not grow weary; they will walk and not tire out." —Isaiah 40:31

Reflection Question: What obstacles are hindering you from living your purpose, and what steps can you take today to overcome them?

July 19th: Connecting with Like-Minded People

Surrounding yourself with like-minded people can support and inspire you on your journey. Today, focus on building connections with those who share your values and passions.

Reach out to someone who inspires you or join a group or community that aligns with your interests. Engage in meaningful conversations and share your goals and aspirations.

Notice the encouragement and motivation that comes from these connections. Recognize the importance of community in pursuing your purpose.

Words of Wisdom: "Find a group of people who challenge and inspire you; spend a lot of time with them, and it will change your life." —Amy Poehler

From the Bible: "Two are better than one because they have a good reward for their hard work. For if one of them falls, the other can help his partner up." —Ecclesiastes 4:9-10

Reflection Question: Who can you connect with today to support and inspire your journey, and how can these connections help you align with your purpose?

July 20th: Reflecting on Progress

Reflecting on your progress helps you stay motivated and focused. Today, take time to review the steps you've taken toward aligning with your purpose and passion.

Think about the actions you've taken, the obstacles you've overcome, and the passions you've nurtured. Celebrate your achievements and recognize your growth.

Write down your reflections and set new goals for the future. Use this reflection as a tool to stay committed to your path.

Words of Wisdom: "Reflect upon your present blessings, of which every man has plenty; not on your past misfortunes, of which all men have some." —Charles Dickens

From the Bible: "Therefore, my beloved brothers, be steadfast, immovable, always having plenty to do in the work of the Lord, knowing that your labor is not in vain in connection with the Lord." —1 Corinthians 15:58

Reflection Question: What progress have you made in aligning with your purpose, and what new goals can you set for the future?

July 21st: Embracing the Journey

Embracing the journey of aligning with your purpose and passion is essential for lasting fulfillment. Today, focus on appreciating the process and being present in each moment.

Reflect on your journey so far. Acknowledge the ups and downs, the lessons learned, and the growth experienced. Embrace the journey as an integral part of living your purpose.

Commit to being present and fully engaged in your daily actions. Recognize that every step, no matter how small, contributes to your overall fulfillment.

Words of Wisdom: "The journey itself is my home." —Matsuo Basho

From the Bible: "Your word is a lamp to my foot, and a light for my path." —Psalm 119:105

Reflection Question: How can you embrace and appreciate your journey today, recognizing that every step is part of living your purpose and passion?

Week 4: Celebrating Self-Expression

Celebrating self-expression is about embracing and showcasing your true self. This week, we focus on the importance of individuality and the joy of expressing who you are. Personal authenticity is a powerful source of peace and fulfillment, allowing you to live in harmony with your values and passions. By celebrating your uniqueness and sharing it with the world, you contribute to a more vibrant and diverse community. Each day's devotion will guide you in exploring and celebrating different aspects of self-expression, helping you to find peace and joy in being authentically you.

July 22nd: Embracing Your Unique Voice

Your unique voice is a powerful tool for self-expression. Today, focus on embracing and sharing your thoughts, ideas, and feelings.

Spend some time reflecting on what makes your perspective unique. Consider your experiences, values, and passions. Write down your thoughts and think about how you can express them more fully.

Celebrate your voice by sharing it with others. Speak up in a conversation, write a blog post, or create something that reflects your unique perspective.

Words of Wisdom: "Do not follow where the path may lead. Go instead where there is no path and leave a trail." —Ralph Waldo Emerson

From the Bible: "Let your words always be gracious, seasoned with salt, so that you will know how you should answer each person." — Colossians 4:6

Reflection Question: How can you embrace and share your unique voice today, and what impact does this have on your sense of authenticity?

July 23rd: Expressing Through Art

Art is a wonderful way to express your inner world. Today, focus on using art to showcase your individuality and creativity.

Choose an art form that resonates with you—drawing, painting, photography, or any other medium. Allow yourself to create freely without worrying about perfection.

Notice how expressing yourself through art brings a sense of joy and fulfillment. Embrace the beauty of your unique creations.

Words of Wisdom: "Art is not what you see, but what you make others see." —Edgar Degas

From the Bible: "He has filled them with skill to do all the work of a craftsman, an embroiderer in blue, purple, and scarlet material, and fine linen, and a weaver, makers of every sort of work and designers." —Exodus 35:35

Reflection Question: What art form can you use today to express your individuality, and how does creating art make you feel?

July 24th: Fashion as Self-Expression

The way you dress can be a powerful form of self-expression. Today, focus on using fashion to reflect your personality and mood.

Take time to choose an outfit that makes you feel confident and true to yourself. Consider colors, patterns, and styles that resonate with who you are.

Notice how dressing authentically impacts your confidence and how others perceive you. Embrace fashion as a fun and meaningful way to express your unique self.

Words of Wisdom: "Fashion is about something that comes from within you." —Ralph Lauren

From the Bible: "She is clothed with strength and splendor, and she looks to the future with confidence." —Proverbs 31:25

Reflection Question: How can you use fashion to express your individuality today, and what impact does this have on your confidence and self-perception?

July 25th: Sharing Your Story

Your life story is a unique and valuable expression of who you are. Today, focus on sharing your story with others.

Think about a significant experience or lesson from your life. Consider how sharing this story could inspire or help others. Write it down or share it verbally with someone you trust.

Notice the connection and understanding that sharing your story creates. Embrace the power of your experiences to make a positive impact on others.

Words of Wisdom: "Only when you are willing to be absolutely vulnerable, you can be absolutely authentic." — Sadhguru

From the Bible: "I will announce your name to my brothers; in the midst of the congregation, I will praise you." —Psalm 22:22

Reflection Question: What part of your story can you share today, and how might it inspire or help someone else?

July 26th: Embodying Authenticity

Living authentically means being true to yourself in all aspects of life. Today, focus on embodying authenticity in your actions and interactions.

Reflect on areas of your life where you feel most authentic and areas where you might be holding back. Consider why this is and how you can be more true to yourself.

Take a step today to be more authentic. Whether it's being honest in a conversation, pursuing a passion, or simply being yourself, notice how it feels to live authentically.

Words of Wisdom: "Being authentic means you have no fear of who you are. Authenticity is about being yourself, even if others may not understand or accept you."— Sadhguru

From the Bible: "But let each one examine his own actions, and then he will have cause for rejoicing in regard to himself alone, and not in comparison with the other person." — Galatians 6:4

Reflection Question: How can you embody more authenticity in your life today, and what impact does this have on your well-being?

July 27th: Celebrating Diversity

Celebrating the diversity of others enriches our lives and broadens our perspectives. Today, focus on appreciating and celebrating the uniqueness of those around you.

Take time to learn about someone else's culture, experiences, or viewpoints. Engage in a conversation, read a book, or watch a documentary that broadens your understanding.

Notice how celebrating diversity enhances your appreciation for the richness of human experience. Embrace the beauty of our differences and the unity it brings.

Words of Wisdom: "We all live with the objective of being happy; our lives are all different and yet the same." —Anne Frank

From the Bible: "For just as the body is one but has many members, and all the members of that body, although many, are one body, so too is the Christ." —1 Corinthians 12:12

Reflection Question: How can you celebrate the diversity of those around you today, and what new perspectives can you gain from this appreciation?

July 28th: Finding Joy in Self-Expression

Self-expression should be a source of joy and freedom. Today, focus on finding joy in expressing your true self in whatever way feels right for you.

Engage in an activity that makes you feel truly yourself—whether it's a hobby, a conversation, or simply spending time alone. Let yourself be fully immersed and enjoy the experience.

Notice the joy that comes from being authentic and expressing yourself freely. Embrace this feeling as a testament to the power of self-expression.

Words of Wisdom: "Your work is to discover your world and then with all your heart give yourself to it." —Gautama Buddha

From the Bible: "The orders from Jehovah are righteous, causing the heart to rejoice." —Psalm 19:8

Reflection Question: What activity brings you the most joy in self-expression, and how can you make time for it today?

July 29th: Expressing Through Movement

Movement is a powerful form of self-expression. Today, focus on expressing yourself through physical activity, whether it's dance, yoga, or any other form of movement.

Choose a type of movement that you enjoy and that allows you to express your emotions and energy. Let your body move freely and naturally, without self-judgment.

Notice how movement helps you release stress and connect with your inner self. Embrace the joy and freedom that comes from expressing yourself through movement.

Words of Wisdom: "Dance is the hidden language of the soul." — Martha Graham

From the Bible: "Praise his name with dancing, accompanied by tambourine and harp." —Psalm 149:3

Reflection Question: How can you express yourself through movement today, and what feelings and emotions do you release in the process?

July 30th: Using Your Creative Talents

Everyone has creative talents that can be used for self-expression. Today, focus on using your unique creative abilities to express yourself and share your gifts with others.

Think about the creative talents you have—writing, painting, cooking, or any other skill. Choose one and spend time today using it to create something meaningful.

Notice how using your talents brings a sense of accomplishment and fulfillment. Embrace the joy of sharing your creativity with the world.

Words of Wisdom: "You can't use up creativity. The more you use, the more you have." —Maya Angelou

From the Bible: "As each one has received a gift, use it in ministering to one another as good stewards of God's undeserved kindness." —1 Peter 4:10

Reflection Question: What creative talent can you use today to express yourself, and how can you share this gift with others?

July 31st: Reflecting on Your Journey

Reflecting on your journey of self-expression helps you appreciate your growth and achievements. Today, focus on looking back at how you've embraced and celebrated your individuality this month.

Think about the ways you've expressed yourself—through art, words, movement, or any other form. Reflect on how these activities have enhanced your sense of authenticity and joy.

Celebrate your progress and commit to continuing your journey of self-expression. Recognize that being true to yourself is a lifelong process that brings peace and fulfillment.

Words of Wisdom: "The privilege of a lifetime is to become who you truly are." —Carl Jung

From the Bible: "But let each one examine his own actions, and then he will have cause for rejoicing in regard to himself alone, and not in comparison with the other person." —Galatians 6:4

Reflection Question: How have you grown in your self-expression this month, and what steps will you take to continue celebrating your individuality?

August: Nourishing the Soul

August is a time to slow down, reflect, and focus on nourishing your soul. As summer begins to wind down, it's the perfect moment to turn inward and prioritize your inner well-being. This month, we will explore practices that bring peace, encourage reflection, and deepen self-care. By taking the time to nurture our souls, we can rejuvenate our spirits, gain clarity, and cultivate a sense of inner peace. Each week will guide you through different aspects of soul nourishment, from self-care rituals to connecting with inner wisdom and releasing self-limiting beliefs. Let's embark on this journey to enrich our inner lives and embrace the tranquility and fulfillment that come from caring for our souls.

Week 1: Basking in Self-Care Rituals

Self-care is essential for nourishing the soul and maintaining a sense of peace and well-being. This week, we focus on incorporating self-care rituals into our daily lives, offering opportunities to slow down, reflect, and rejuvenate. By engaging in practices like meditation, yoga, nature walks, and other calming activities, we can foster a deeper connection with ourselves and cultivate inner tranquility. Each day's devotion will suggest a different self-care ritual, encouraging you to explore what brings you the most peace and well-being. Let's take this time to prioritize our inner health and embrace the soothing benefits of self-care.

August 1st: Morning Meditation

Starting your day with meditation can set a peaceful tone for the hours ahead. Today, focus on incorporating a morning meditation practice into your routine.

Find a quiet spot where you can sit comfortably. Close your eyes and take deep breaths, focusing on the sensation of the air entering and leaving your body. Allow your mind to settle and gently release any thoughts that arise.

Spend at least ten minutes in this meditative state. Notice the sense of calm and clarity that follows, carrying this tranquility with you throughout the day.

Words of Wisdom: "Meditation is a practice that transforms confusion into clarity." —Pema Chodron

From the Bible: "Jehovah is near to all those calling on him, to all who call on him in truth." —Psalm 145:18

Reflection Question: How does starting your day with meditation impact your overall sense of peace and well-being?

August 2nd: Yoga for Inner Calm

Yoga combines physical movement with mindfulness, promoting both physical and mental well-being. Today, focus on practicing yoga to cultivate inner calm and flexibility.

Choose a series of yoga poses that resonate with you, whether it's a gentle flow or a more vigorous practice. Pay attention to your breath and how your body feels with each movement.

Notice how yoga helps release tension and brings a sense of peace and centeredness. Embrace the connection between your body and mind, appreciating the balance it brings.

Words of Wisdom: "Yoga is a journey toward creating harmony within the body and mind." —Sadhguru

From the Bible: "For God has not given us a spirit of cowardice, but one of power and of love and of soundness of mind." —2 Timothy 1:7

Reflection Question: How does practicing yoga help you connect with your body and mind, and what benefits do you notice?

August 3rd: Nature Walks for Reflection

Spending time in nature is a powerful way to nourish the soul. Today, focus on taking a walk in a natural setting to reflect and rejuvenate.

Find a nearby park, forest, or beach where you can walk peacefully. As you walk, pay attention to the sights, sounds, and smells around you. Let nature's beauty fill your senses.

Use this time to reflect on your thoughts and feelings, allowing the natural environment to bring you clarity and peace. Notice how nature's tranquility enhances your sense of well-being.

Words of Wisdom: "When you walk in nature, you find the rhythm of your soul." —Michael Singer

From the Bible: "The earth is Jehovah's, and everything in it, the productive land and those dwelling on it." —Psalm 24:1

Reflection Question: How does spending time in nature help you reflect and rejuvenate, and what insights do you gain from this experience?

August 4th: Mindful Breathing

Mindful breathing is a simple yet effective way to calm the mind and reduce stress. Today, focus on practicing mindful breathing to bring peace and relaxation.

Sit or lie down in a comfortable position. Close your eyes and take slow, deep breaths, focusing on the sensation of the air entering and leaving your lungs. If your mind wanders, gently bring your focus back to your breath.

Spend at least five minutes in this practice. Notice how mindful breathing helps you feel more centered and at ease, reducing stress and promoting a sense of well-being.

Words of Wisdom: "Mindful breathing is the foundation of emotional and physical well-being." —Thich Nhat Hanh

From the Bible: "The spirit of man is the lamp of Jehovah, searching all his innermost parts." —Proverbs 20:27

Reflection Question: How does mindful breathing help you reduce stress and find inner peace, and how can you incorporate this practice into your daily routine?

August 5th: Journaling for Clarity

Journaling is a powerful tool for self-reflection and clarity. Today, focus on writing in a journal to explore your thoughts and feelings.

Set aside time to write freely about whatever comes to mind. Reflect on your day, your emotions, or any challenges you're facing. Allow your writing to flow without judgment or editing.

Notice how journaling helps you gain insights and clarity about your inner world. Embrace this practice as a way to connect with yourself and understand your thoughts and emotions more deeply.

Words of Wisdom: "Through journaling, we connect with the voice within that speaks our truth." —Lynne McTaggart

From the Bible: "The purposes of a man's heart are deep waters, but a man of understanding draws them out." —Proverbs 20:5

Reflection Question: How does journaling help you gain clarity and understand your thoughts and emotions, and what benefits do you notice from this practice?

August 6th: Listening to Soothing Music

Music has the power to soothe the soul and elevate your mood. Today, focus on listening to soothing music that brings you peace and relaxation.

Choose a playlist or album of calming music—classical, instrumental, or nature sounds. Find a quiet place to sit or lie down, close your eyes, and let the music wash over you.

Notice how the music affects your mood and stress levels. Allow yourself to fully relax and enjoy the peaceful sounds, appreciating the tranquility they bring.

Words of Wisdom: "Music touches us emotionally, where words alone can't." —Wayne Dyer

From the Bible: "Praise Jehovah with the harp; make melody to him on a ten-stringed instrument." —Psalm 33:2

Reflection Question: How does listening to soothing music impact your mood and stress levels, and how can you make time for this practice in your daily life?

August 7th: Creating a Self-Care Sanctuary

Having a dedicated space for self-care can enhance your well-being. Today, focus on creating a self-care sanctuary in your home.

Choose a space that you can dedicate to relaxation and self-care. Decorate it with items that bring you joy and peace—candles, cushions, plants, or art. Make it a place where you can retreat to recharge.

Spend time in your self-care sanctuary today, engaging in a calming activity such as reading, meditating, or simply resting. Notice how having this space enhances your sense of peace and well-being.

Words of Wisdom: "Your environment can be a place of renewal and reflection." —Rhonda Byrne

From the Bible: "He makes me lie down in green pastures; He leads me beside quiet waters." —Psalm 23:2

Reflection Question: How can you create a self-care sanctuary in your home, and what activities can you engage in to make the most of this space?

Week 2: Connecting with Inner Wisdom

Connecting with your inner wisdom involves tuning into your inner voice and trusting your intuition. This week, we focus on introspection and the ways we can listen to and honor our inner guidance. By creating space for quiet reflection and mindfulness, we can hear the subtle messages that guide us toward our true path. Each day's devotion will provide practices and insights to help you connect with your inner wisdom, offering guidance on listening to your inner cues and intuitions. Embrace this journey of self-discovery and trust the wisdom that lies within you.

August 8th: Listening to Your Inner Voice

Your inner voice is a powerful source of guidance. Today, focus on creating a quiet space to listen to what your inner self is telling you.

Find a peaceful place where you can sit quietly. Close your eyes, take deep breaths, and ask yourself a question that's been on your mind. Listen patiently for any thoughts, feelings, or images that arise.

Notice how your inner voice speaks to you and the clarity it brings. Trust that your intuition has valuable insights to offer.

Words of Wisdom: "Stillness is where creativity and solutions to problems are found." —Eckhart Tolle

From the Bible: "And your own ears will hear a word behind you saying, 'This is the way. Walk in it,' whether you go to the right or to the left." —Isaiah 30:21

Reflection Question: What question do you need guidance on today, and how can you create space to listen to your inner voice?

August 9th: Meditating for Insight

Meditation helps quiet the mind and connect with inner wisdom. Today, focus on a meditation practice that invites insight and clarity.

Sit in a comfortable position and close your eyes. Take slow, deep breaths, and allow your mind to settle. Visualize a peaceful place where you feel safe and calm. Ask your inner self for guidance on a specific issue and remain open to any thoughts or feelings that arise.

Reflect on any insights you receive during your meditation. Trust that your inner wisdom is guiding you toward the answers you seek.

Words of Wisdom: "Meditation is a journey inward, leading to the discovery of your own truth." —Dr. Joe Dispenza

From the Bible: "For wisdom is a protection just as money is a protection, but the advantage of knowledge is this: Wisdom preserves the life of its owner." —Ecclesiastes 7:12

Reflection Question: How can meditation help you connect with your inner wisdom, and what insights have you gained from this practice?

August 10th: Journaling for Inner Guidance

Journaling can be a powerful way to connect with your inner wisdom. Today, focus on writing to uncover insights and guidance from within.

Set aside time to write freely about any questions or challenges you're facing. Let your thoughts flow without judgment or editing. Pay attention to any recurring themes or surprising insights that emerge.

Reflect on your journal entries and consider how they align with your inner guidance. Trust that writing can help you access deeper layers of wisdom.

Words of Wisdom: "The act of writing lets your inner wisdom surface." —Pema Chodron

From the Bible: "For Jehovah gives wisdom; from his mouth come knowledge and discernment." —Proverbs 2:6

Reflection Question: How does journaling help you uncover inner guidance, and what insights have you discovered through this practice?

August 11th: Trusting Your Gut Feelings

Your gut feelings are often a manifestation of your inner wisdom. Today, focus on paying attention to and trusting these intuitive cues.

Reflect on a situation where you had a strong gut feeling. How did it guide you? Consider any current situations where your intuition is giving you clear signals.

Act on one of your gut feelings today. Notice how trusting your intuition affects the outcome and your sense of confidence.

Words of Wisdom: "Intuition is your soul speaking to you, guiding you on the path of truth." —Michael Singer

From the Bible: "A man of discernment keeps quiet." —Proverbs 11:12

Reflection Question: How can you trust your gut feelings more today, and what current situation can you apply this to?

August 12th: Seeking Solitude for Clarity

Solitude can provide the clarity needed to connect with your inner wisdom. Today, focus on spending time alone to gain insight and understanding.

Find a quiet place where you can be alone with your thoughts. Reflect on any questions or decisions you're facing. Allow the stillness to bring clarity and insight.

Notice how solitude helps you connect with your true self and your inner guidance. Embrace the peace and clarity that come from spending time alone.

Words of Wisdom: "Solitude is the gateway to self-discovery and inner peace." —Sadhguru

From the Bible: "But Jesus often withdrew to lonely places and prayed." —Luke 5:16

Reflection Question: How can you seek solitude today to gain clarity, and what insights do you hope to uncover during this time alone?

August 13th: Learning from Past Experiences

Reflecting on past experiences can reveal patterns and lessons that guide your future actions. Today, focus on learning from your past to connect with your inner wisdom.

Think about a significant past experience. What did it teach you about yourself and your values? How can this lesson guide you in your current situation?

Write down the insights you've gained from reflecting on your past. Use these lessons as a compass for your future decisions and actions.

Words of Wisdom: "Every experience is a lesson, every loss is a gain." —ACIM

From the Bible: "Remember the days of old; consider the years of past generations." —Deuteronomy 32:7

Reflection Question: What past experience can you reflect on today to gain insight, and how can this lesson guide your current actions?

August 14th: Aligning Actions with Inner Wisdom

Aligning your actions with your inner wisdom leads to a more authentic and fulfilling life. Today, focus on making decisions and taking actions that reflect your true self.

Identify a decision you need to make or an action you need to take. Reflect on what your inner wisdom is guiding you to do. Consider the long-term impact of aligning your actions with your true values and desires.

Take a step today that aligns with your inner wisdom. Notice how this decision enhances your sense of authenticity and peace.

Words of Wisdom: "True wisdom is living in harmony with your deepest values." —Wayne Dyer

From the Bible: "Make me know your ways, O Jehovah; teach me your paths." —Psalm 25:4

Reflection Question: What action can you take today that aligns with your inner wisdom, and how does this decision contribute to a more authentic and fulfilling life?

Week 3: Releasing Self-Limiting Beliefs

Self-limiting beliefs are those thoughts and attitudes that hold us back from achieving our full potential and living authentically. This week, we focus on identifying and releasing these beliefs to foster personal peace and self-expression. By recognizing the negative patterns in our thinking, we can challenge and transform them, allowing us to embrace our true capabilities and live more freely. Each day's devotion will guide you through practices to uncover and let go of self-limiting beliefs, inspiring you to live a life that reflects your true self and values.

August 15th: Identifying Self-Limiting Beliefs

The first step in overcoming self-limiting beliefs is to identify them. Today, focus on recognizing the thoughts and attitudes that hold you back.

Reflect on a goal or dream that you've struggled to achieve. What thoughts or beliefs come up when you think about pursuing this goal? Write them down and examine their origins.

Notice how these beliefs influence your actions and decisions. Recognize that identifying them is the first step toward overcoming them.

Words of Wisdom: "Your beliefs shape your reality. Choose them wisely." —Lynne McTaggart

From the Bible: "For as he thinks in his heart, so he is." —Proverbs 23:7

Reflection Question: What self-limiting beliefs can you identify today, and how have they impacted your goals and dreams?

August 16th: Challenging Negative Thoughts

Once you've identified self-limiting beliefs, the next step is to challenge them. Today, focus on questioning the validity of these negative thoughts.

Take one self-limiting belief you identified yesterday. Ask yourself: Is this belief based on fact or assumption? What evidence supports or contradicts it?

Write down your findings and consider a more positive and inspiring belief to replace the negative one. Challenge yourself to adopt this new perspective.

Words of Wisdom: "The only limits that exist are those you place on yourself." —Sadhguru

From the Bible: "We are bringing every thought into captivity to make it obedient to the Christ." —2 Corinthians 10:5

Reflection Question: How can you challenge a self-limiting belief today, and what new, inspiring belief can you adopt instead?

August 17th: Affirming Your Strengths

Affirmations can help replace self-limiting beliefs with positive ones. Today, focus on affirming your strengths and capabilities.

Write down a list of your strengths and accomplishments. Choose a few positive affirmations that resonate with you, such as "I am capable," "I am deserving of success," or "I have the power to create positive change."

Repeat these affirmations throughout the day, especially when you notice self-limiting thoughts arising. Embrace the power of positive self-talk to transform your mindset.

Words of Wisdom: "Affirmation is the bridge between where you are and where you want to be." —Rhonda Byrne

From the Bible: "For all things I have the strength through the one who gives me power." —Philippians 4:13

Reflection Question: What positive affirmations can you use today to counteract self-limiting beliefs, and how do these affirmations make you feel?

August 18th: Visualizing Success

Visualization is a powerful tool for overcoming self-limiting beliefs. Today, focus on visualizing your success and achieving your goals.

Find a quiet place to sit comfortably. Close your eyes and visualize yourself achieving a goal you've set. Imagine every detail—how you feel, what you see, who is with you.

Spend a few minutes each day visualizing your success. Notice how this practice boosts your confidence and motivates you to take action.

Words of Wisdom: "See yourself living in abundance and you will attract it." —Rhonda Byrne

From the Bible: "For we are walking by faith, not by sight." —2 Corinthians 5:7

Reflection Question: How can visualizing your success help you overcome self-limiting beliefs, and what specific goal can you focus on today?

August 19th: Embracing Failure as Growth

Fear of failure often underpins self-limiting beliefs. Today, focus on embracing failure as an opportunity for growth and learning.

Reflect on a past failure and what you learned from it. How did this experience help you grow? Write down the lessons and how they have contributed to your personal development.

Shift your perspective on failure. See it as a stepping stone to success rather than a setback. Embrace the growth and resilience that come from overcoming challenges.

Words of Wisdom: "Failure is not the opposite of success; it's part of success." —Michael Singer

From the Bible: "The righteous one may fall seven times, and he will get up again." —Proverbs 24:16

Reflection Question: How can you reframe a past failure as a growth opportunity, and what lessons have you learned that can help you move forward?

August 20th: Surrounding Yourself with Positivity

Your environment influences your beliefs and mindset. Today, focus on surrounding yourself with positive influences that uplift and inspire you.

Think about the people, media, and activities that fill your life. Are they positive and supportive? Seek out friends, mentors, and content that encourage growth and positivity.

Notice the impact of a positive environment on your mindset and self-belief. Embrace the power of positivity to transform your life and release self-limiting beliefs.

Words of Wisdom: "The energy around you shapes your reality. Surround yourself with positivity." —Dr. Joe Dispenza

From the Bible: "Do not be misled. Bad associations spoil useful habits." —1 Corinthians 15:33

Reflection Question: How can you create a more positive environment in your life, and what changes can you make to support this shift?

August 21st: Committing to Continuous Growth

Releasing self-limiting beliefs is an ongoing process. Today, focus on committing to continuous growth and self-improvement.

Set a personal growth goal for yourself. It could be reading a book on self-improvement, attending a workshop, or practicing a new skill. Make a plan to achieve this goal.

Reflect on your journey so far and celebrate your progress. Embrace the commitment to lifelong learning and growth, knowing that each step forward brings you closer to your true potential.

Words of Wisdom: "Growth is the only evidence of life." —John Henry Newman

From the Bible: "But the path of the righteous is like the bright morning light that grows brighter and brighter until full daylight." —Proverbs 4:18

Reflection Question: What personal growth goal can you set for yourself today, and how will this commitment help you continue releasing self-limiting beliefs?

Week 4: Radiating Love and Compassion

As we conclude the summer theme, let's focus on extending love and compassion outward, reinforcing the idea that what we give is reflected back to us. Radiating love and compassion not only enriches the lives of those around us but also brings profound joy and fulfillment to our own hearts. This week, we will explore ways to cultivate and share these qualities, understanding that acts of kindness and empathy create a ripple effect, enhancing the well-being of our communities and ourselves. Each day's devotion will guide you in embracing and expressing love and compassion in your daily life.

August 22nd: Acts of Kindness

Simple acts of kindness can have a profound impact. Today, focus on performing a random act of kindness for someone.

Think about a small gesture that can make someone's day brighter—buying a coffee for a stranger, helping a neighbor with groceries, or sending an encouraging note.

Notice the joy and connection that result from your act of kindness. Recognize that these small actions create positive energy that spreads beyond the immediate moment.

Words of Wisdom: "A single act of kindness throws out roots in all directions." —Amelia Earhart

From the Bible: "But besides all these things, clothe yourselves with love, for it is a perfect bond of union." —Colossians 3:14

Reflection Question: What act of kindness can you perform today, and how does it impact both you and the recipient?

August 23rd: Listening with Compassion

Listening is one of the greatest gifts we can give. Today, focus on being fully present and listening with compassion.

When someone speaks to you, give them your undivided attention. Listen without interrupting, judging, or offering solutions. Just be there to understand and support.

Notice how this compassionate listening deepens your connection with others. Recognize the healing power of being truly heard.

Words of Wisdom: "When you listen with empathy, you nurture understanding and compassion." —Pema Chodron

From the Bible: "The one guarding his mouth preserves his life; the one opening his lips wide comes to ruin." —Proverbs 13:3

Reflection Question: How can you practice compassionate listening today, and what difference does it make in your interactions?

August 24th: Spreading Positivity

Positivity is contagious. Today, focus on spreading positive energy through your words and actions.

Start by expressing gratitude to those around you. Compliment a colleague, thank a family member, or encourage a friend. Let your positivity shine through genuine and uplifting interactions.

Notice how spreading positivity enhances your own mood and the atmosphere around you. Recognize the power of positive energy in transforming your day.

Words of Wisdom: "Your positive energy is contagious. Let it ripple out into the world." —Rhonda Byrne

From the Bible: "A soothing tongue is a tree of life, but a deceitful tongue crushes the spirit." —Proverbs 15:4

Reflection Question: How can you spread positivity today, and what impact does it have on you and those around you?

August 25th: Offering Help and Support

Offering help and support to others strengthens our sense of community. Today, focus on being there for someone in need.

Think about a person in your life who could use some support. Reach out and offer your help, whether it's through a listening ear, a helping hand, or some practical assistance.

Notice how offering support fosters a sense of connection and purpose. Recognize the mutual benefits of helping and being helped.

Words of Wisdom: "The greatest gift you can give someone is your presence and support." —Wayne Dyer

From the Bible: "Let each one keep seeking, not his own advantage, but that of the other person." —1 Corinthians 10:24

Reflection Question: Who can you offer help and support to today, and how does this act of compassion affect your relationship?

August 26th: Practicing Forgiveness

Forgiveness frees us from the burdens of resentment and anger. Today, focus on practicing forgiveness toward yourself and others.

Reflect on any grudges or negative feelings you're holding onto. Consider the impact of these feelings on your well-being. Choose to let go and forgive, recognizing that forgiveness is a gift to yourself.

Notice the sense of relief and peace that follows. Embrace the freedom and healing that come with forgiveness.

Words of Wisdom: "Forgiveness is the key to inner peace because it is the mental technique by which our thoughts are transformed." —ACIM

From the Bible: "If you forgive others their trespasses, your heavenly Father will also forgive you." —Matthew 6:14

Reflection Question: What grievances can you forgive today, and how does this act of forgiveness bring you peace?

August 27th: Connecting with Nature

Nature has a unique way of nurturing our sense of love and compassion. Today, focus on spending time in nature to reconnect with these feelings.

Take a walk in a park, hike in the woods, or simply sit by a body of water. Observe the beauty and tranquility around you. Let the natural world remind you of the interconnectedness of all life.

Notice how nature enhances your sense of compassion for all living things. Recognize the healing and unifying power of the natural world.

Words of Wisdom: "Nature is a reflection of the soul; find peace in its embrace." —Sadhguru

From the Bible: "The heavens are declaring the glory of God; the skies above proclaim the work of his hands." —Psalm 19:1

Reflection Question: How can spending time in nature today deepen your sense of love and compassion for all living beings?

August 28th: Expressing Gratitude

Gratitude is a powerful way to cultivate love and compassion. Today, focus on expressing gratitude for the people and experiences that bring joy to your life.

Make a list of things you're grateful for. Consider writing a thank-you note to someone who has made a positive impact on your life. Express your appreciation sincerely and openly.

Notice how expressing gratitude enhances your sense of connection and well-being. Embrace the warmth and positivity that come from a grateful heart.

Words of Wisdom: "A grateful heart is a magnet for miracles, drawing blessings into your life with every expression of thanks." —Dr. Joe Dispenza, *Becoming Supernatural*

From the Bible: "Give thanks for everything." —1 Thessalonians 5:18

Reflection Question: What are you grateful for today, and how can you express this gratitude to others?

August 29th: Radiating Love

Radiating love involves embodying and sharing unconditional love with others. Today, focus on being a source of love and light in your interactions.

Reflect on the love you feel for yourself and those around you. Set an intention to radiate this love in your words and actions throughout the day. Smile, offer kind words, and be present for those you encounter.

Notice how radiating love creates a positive and uplifting atmosphere. Recognize the ripple effect of your loving energy.

Words of Wisdom: "Love is not what you do; it's who you are." — Wayne Dyer

From the Bible: "Above all things, have intense love for one another, because love covers a multitude of sins." —1 Peter 4:8

Reflection Question: How can you radiate love in your interactions today, and what impact does this have on those around you?

August 30th: Compassion for Yourself

Compassion for yourself is just as important as compassion for others. Today, focus on extending love and kindness to yourself.

Reflect on how you treat yourself in moments of difficulty. Practice self-compassion by speaking kindly to yourself, acknowledging your efforts, and forgiving your mistakes.

Notice the peace and healing that come from treating yourself with compassion. Embrace the understanding that self-love is the foundation of love for others.

Words of Wisdom: "You cannot give to others what you do not give to yourself." —Pema Chodron

From the Bible: "This is my commandment, that you love one another just as I have loved you." —John 15:12

Reflection Question: What can you do today to nurture self-compassion, and how does it contribute to your sense of peace?

August 31st: Reflecting on Love and Compassion

As we conclude this month, take time to reflect on how you've extended love and compassion outward. Today, focus on reviewing your journey and setting intentions for the future.

Think about the ways you've shown love and compassion this month. What have you learned about yourself and others? Write down your reflections and consider how you can continue to cultivate these qualities.

Celebrate the progress you've made and commit to nurturing love and compassion in your daily life.

Words of Wisdom: "The essence of life is to love and be loved." — Michael Singer

From the Bible: "Now, however, these three remain: faith, hope, love; but the greatest of these is love." —1 Corinthians 13:13

Reflection Question: How have you grown in your ability to radiate love and compassion this month, and what intentions can you set to continue this practice in the future?

Chapter 4: Autumn
Harvest and Gratitude

Autumn is a season of harvest, a time when the fruits of our labor are gathered and celebrated. As the leaves change color and the air turns crisp, we are reminded of the cycles of life—growth, transformation, and the eventual gathering of our efforts. Autumn invites us to reflect on the abundance in our lives, to embrace change, and to cultivate gratitude for the many blessings we've received.

September marks the beginning of the harvest season, a time to cultivate and recognize the abundance in our lives. This month focuses on harvesting gratitude for the many blessings we've received throughout the year. It's a time to embrace the changes and transitions that come with the season, reflecting on the inner harvest—the growth and wisdom gained from our experiences.

As we move into October, the focus shifts to embracing transformation. The vibrant colors of autumn leaves remind us that change is not only inevitable but also beautiful. This month encourages us to embrace the shadows with compassion, to nurture the seeds of transformation, and to align ourselves with inner balance. October is a time to reflect on the beauty of impermanence, understanding that every ending is also a beginning.

November, the final month of autumn, is a time to cultivate inner warmth as we prepare for the winter ahead. This month is about embracing the spirit of gratitude and connecting with the peace that comes from within. It's a time to focus on self-compassion, letting go of any lingering negativity and radiating love and kindness to others. As the days grow shorter and the nights longer, November encourages us to find warmth in our relationships, our communities, and most importantly, within ourselves.

In this chapter, as you journey through the autumn months, you will explore how gratitude, transformation, and kindness can enrich your life. Each devotion is designed to help you harvest the wisdom and blessings of the year, embrace the beauty of change, and cultivate a heart full of warmth and kindness. Through these practices, you will find that autumn is not just a time of gathering but also a season of deepening your connection to the abundance and richness of life.

September: Cultivating Abundance

Autumn is a time of harvest, a season to gather and celebrate the abundance we've cultivated throughout the year. This month, we reflect on the richness in our lives, not just in material terms but also emotionally and spiritually. The crisp air and golden leaves remind us to appreciate the fruits of our labor and the growth we've experienced.

September is an ideal time to express gratitude for the blessings we've received and to share our abundance through acts of kindness. As we recognize the fullness of our lives, we become more aware of the ways we can contribute to the well-being of others. By focusing on the abundance around us and within us, we can cultivate a heart full of gratitude and a spirit of generosity. This month, let's celebrate the harvest of our lives and spread kindness, enriching our own lives and the lives of those around us.

Week 1: Harvesting Gratitude for Abundance

Gratitude is the foundation of a fulfilling life. This week, we focus on harvesting gratitude for the abundance in our lives. By recognizing and appreciating the richness around us—from personal achievements to the beauty of nature—we can cultivate a deeper sense of contentment and joy. Each day's devotion will guide you to explore different aspects of abundance, encouraging you to pause, reflect, and give thanks for the many blessings in your life. Let's start this journey of gratitude and open our hearts to the fullness of our experiences.

September 1st: Appreciating Personal Achievements

Take a moment today to reflect on your personal achievements. Consider the goals you've reached and the progress you've made, no matter how small.

Write down a list of accomplishments from the past year. Celebrate each one and recognize the effort and dedication it took to achieve them.

Notice the sense of pride and gratitude that arises from acknowledging your achievements. Allow this recognition to inspire and motivate you for future endeavors.

Words of Wisdom: "Gratitude turns what we have into enough." — Rhonda Byrne, *The Power*

From the Bible: "Whatever you are doing, work at it whole-souled as for Jehovah, and not for men." —Colossians 3:23

Reflection Question: What personal achievements are you most proud of, and how can you celebrate them today?

September 2nd: Gratitude for Relationships

Today, focus on the abundance found in your relationships. Reflect on the people who bring joy, support, and love into your life.

Think about a few key relationships that have positively impacted you. Consider writing a note of appreciation to someone who has been particularly supportive or loving.

Notice the warmth that comes from expressing gratitude for your connections. Recognize the mutual enrichment that these relationships bring to your life.

Words of Wisdom: "True love and friendship are deeply rooted in appreciation." —Michael Singer, *The Untethered Soul*

From the Bible: "Faithful are the wounds of a friend; profuse are the kisses of an enemy." —Proverbs 27:6

Reflection Question: Who in your life are you grateful for today, and how can you show them your appreciation?

September 3rd: Finding Joy in Nature

Nature offers an endless source of abundance. Today, take time to appreciate the natural beauty around you.

Go for a walk outside, visit a park, or simply sit in your garden. Pay attention to the sights, sounds, and smells of nature. Reflect on the peace and inspiration that come from the natural world.

Notice how connecting with nature enhances your sense of gratitude and well-being. Recognize the abundance of beauty that surrounds you every day.

Words of Wisdom: "In nature, nothing is perfect and everything is perfect. Nature teaches us simplicity and contentment." —Pema Chodron, *Comfortable with Uncertainty*

From the Bible: "For everything created by God is good, and nothing is to be rejected if it is received with gratitude." —1 Timothy 4:4

Reflection Question: How does spending time in nature help you appreciate the abundance in your life?

September 4th: Celebrating Small Joys

Abundance is often found in the small, everyday joys. Today, focus on appreciating the little things that bring happiness to your day.

Make a list of small joys that you experience—your morning coffee, a smile from a stranger, the sound of your favorite song. Take time to savor each of these moments.

Notice how recognizing and celebrating these small joys enhances your overall sense of gratitude and contentment. Embrace the abundance in the little things.

Words of Wisdom: "Appreciate the little things, for they make up the big picture of life." —Lynne McTaggart, *Living the Field*

From the Bible: "You have changed my mourning into dancing; you have removed my sackcloth and clothed me with joy." —Psalm 30:11

Reflection Question: What small joys can you celebrate today, and how do they contribute to your sense of abundance?

September 5th: Gratitude for Learning and Growth

Learning and personal growth are significant sources of abundance. Today, reflect on the knowledge and skills you've acquired over time.

Think about a recent lesson you've learned or a skill you've developed. How has this growth benefited you? Write down your reflections and appreciate the journey of learning.

Notice the pride and satisfaction that come from acknowledging your growth. Recognize the abundance in your continuous journey of self-improvement.

Words of Wisdom: "The more you learn, the more you appreciate the abundance of life." —Wayne Dyer, *There's a Spiritual Solution to Every Problem*

From the Bible: "Let the wise listen and add to their learning, and let the discerning get guidance." —Proverbs 1:5

Reflection Question: What have you learned recently that has enriched your life, and how can you celebrate this growth?

September 6th: Appreciating Health and Well-being

Health is a cornerstone of abundance. Today, focus on appreciating your physical and mental well-being.

Reflect on aspects of your health that you often take for granted. Consider your ability to move, breathe, and think clearly. Write down what you're grateful for in terms of your health.

Notice how focusing on your well-being enhances your gratitude. Recognize the abundance of health and the opportunities it provides.

Words of Wisdom: "Health is the real wealth, and gratitude for it is priceless." —Sadhguru, *Inner Engineering*

From the Bible: "For bodily training is beneficial for a little, but godly devotion is beneficial for all things, as it holds promise of the life now and that which is to come." —1 Timothy 4:8

Reflection Question: What aspects of your health are you grateful for today, and how can you take better care of yourself?

September 7th: Recognizing Community Support

Our communities provide a wealth of support and connection. Today, reflect on the abundance found in your community.

Think about the people and groups that support and uplift you— neighbors, colleagues, local organizations. Take a moment to appreciate their contributions to your life.

Notice the sense of belonging and gratitude that comes from recognizing your community. Embrace the abundance of support and connection around you.

Words of Wisdom: "A strong community is built on the foundation of mutual support and gratitude." —Rhonda Byrne, *The Power*

From the Bible: "Now you are Christ's body, and each of you individually is a member of it." —1 Corinthians 12:27

Reflection Question: How does your community support and enrich your life, and how can you show appreciation for this support?

Week 2: Embracing Change and Transition

Autumn is a season of transformation, marked by the changing colors of leaves and the cooling of temperatures. These natural transitions mirror the changes we experience in our own lives. Embracing change can be challenging, but it also offers opportunities for growth and renewal. This week, we will explore how to welcome transitions with a positive mindset and extend kindness to ourselves and others during these times. Each day's devotion will guide you in understanding and navigating change, helping you find strength and grace in the midst of transformation.

September 8th: Welcoming New Beginnings

Change often brings new beginnings. Today, focus on welcoming the new opportunities and experiences that come with change.

Reflect on a recent change in your life. What new opportunities has it brought? Write down how these new beginnings can contribute to your personal growth.

Embrace the excitement and potential that come with new beginnings. Trust that each change is a stepping stone to a richer, more fulfilling life.

Words of Wisdom: "Every new beginning comes from some other beginning's end." —Michael Singer, *The Untethered Soul*

From the Bible: "See, I am creating new heavens and a new earth; and the former things will not be called to mind, nor will they come up into the heart." —Isaiah 65:17

Reflection Question: What new beginnings can you embrace today, and how can they contribute to your growth?

September 9th: Letting Go with Grace

Letting go is a crucial part of embracing change. Today, focus on releasing what no longer serves you with grace and kindness.

Think about something you need to let go of—a habit, a relationship, a fear. Write down the reasons why letting go will benefit you.

Acknowledge the emotions that come with letting go, and be kind to yourself during this process. Recognize that releasing the old makes room for new growth.

Words of Wisdom: "Letting go is the first step towards new beginnings." —Pema Chodron, *Comfortable with Uncertainty*

From the Bible: "Cast your burden on Jehovah, and he will sustain you." —Psalm 55:22

Reflection Question: What do you need to let go of today, and how can you do so with grace and kindness?

September 10th: Embracing Uncertainty

Uncertainty is a natural part of change. Today, focus on embracing uncertainty with an open heart and mind.

Reflect on a situation where you feel uncertain. Write down the potential positives that could come from this uncertainty. Consider how it might lead to unexpected opportunities.

Trust that uncertainty is a part of the growth process. Embrace it as a chance to explore new possibilities and learn more about yourself.

Words of Wisdom: "In uncertainty, there is the potential for boundless possibilities." —Lynne McTaggart, *Living the Field*

From the Bible: "Trust in Jehovah and do good; reside in the earth, and act in faithfulness." —Psalm 37:3

Reflection Question: How can you embrace uncertainty today, and what potential positives can come from it?

September 11th: Finding Stability in Change

Even in the midst of change, we can find stability. Today, focus on the constants in your life that provide a sense of grounding.

Identify the aspects of your life that remain stable during times of change—family, faith, routines. Write down how these constants support you.

Lean on these stable elements as you navigate transitions. Recognize the balance between change and stability in your life.

Words of Wisdom: "Change is the only constant, but within you lies a steadfast spirit." —Sadhguru, *Inner Engineering*

From the Bible: "For I am Jehovah; I do not change." —Malachi 3:6

Reflection Question: What constants in your life provide stability, and how can you lean on them during times of change?

September 12th: Being Kind to Yourself

Change can be stressful, and it's important to be kind to yourself during these times. Today, focus on self-compassion.

Reflect on how you treat yourself during times of change. Write down ways you can be kinder to yourself—positive self-talk, taking breaks, seeking support.

Practice self-compassion today. Recognize that it's okay to struggle with change and that being kind to yourself will help you navigate it more effectively.

Words of Wisdom: "Self-compassion is the foundation of inner strength and resilience." —Pema Chodron, *Comfortable with Uncertainty*

From the Bible: "Do not withhold good from those to whom it is due, when it is in your power to act." —Proverbs 3:27

Reflection Question: How can you be kinder to yourself today, and what specific actions can you take to practice self-compassion?

September 13th: Supporting Others Through Change

Supporting others during times of change fosters connection and community. Today, focus on how you can be a source of support for those around you.

Think about someone in your life who is going through a transition. Write down ways you can support them—listening, offering help, or simply being there.

Reach out to this person today. Show your support and let them know they are not alone in their journey.

Words of Wisdom: "When we support each other, we build a stronger, more compassionate world." —Wayne Dyer, *There's a Spiritual Solution to Every Problem*

From the Bible: "A cord of three strands is not quickly broken." —Ecclesiastes 4:12

Reflection Question: Who can you support today, and how can you show your kindness and compassion?

September 14th: Embracing the Present Moment

Living in the present moment helps us embrace change with grace. Today, focus on being fully present in your daily activities.

Practice mindfulness in whatever you do today—eating, walking, working. Pay attention to the details and sensations of the present moment.

Notice how being present helps you appreciate the here and now, making it easier to navigate transitions with a calm and centered mindset.

Words of Wisdom: "The present moment is the gateway to peace." —Michael Singer, *The Untethered Soul*

From the Bible: "So never be anxious about the next day, for the next day will have its own anxieties." —Matthew 6:34

Reflection Question: How can you practice mindfulness today, and how does being present help you embrace change?

Week 3: Reflecting on Inner Harvest

Autumn is a time to reflect on the inner harvest of personal growth and development. As we look back on the past year, we can appreciate the lessons learned, the challenges overcome, and the ways we have evolved. This week, we will explore our inner harvest, considering the insights gained and the strengths developed. By reflecting on our personal growth, we can celebrate our progress and set intentions for continued growth and transformation. Each day's devotion will guide you in this reflective practice, drawing on wisdom from various spiritual and self-help sources.

September 15th: Recognizing Personal Growth

Reflecting on personal growth allows us to appreciate our journey and recognize our progress. Today, focus on acknowledging how far you've come this year.

Think about a challenge you faced this year. What did you learn from it? How did you grow stronger or wiser? Write down your reflections.

Celebrate your growth and recognize the effort you've put into becoming who you are today.

Words of Wisdom: "Growth begins when we start to accept our own weakness." —Pema Chodron, *Comfortable with Uncertainty*

From the Bible: "Consider it all joy, my brothers, when you meet with various trials, knowing as you do that this tested quality of your faith produces endurance." —James 1:2-3

Reflection Question: What challenge did you overcome this year, and how did it contribute to your personal growth?

September 16th: Learning from Difficulties

Difficulties are often our greatest teachers. Today, focus on the lessons learned from the tough times.

Reflect on a difficult period from this year. What did you learn about yourself and your resilience? Write down the insights you gained.

Acknowledge the wisdom that comes from facing and overcoming difficulties. Embrace the strength you've developed through these experiences.

Words of Wisdom: "The lessons we learn in adversity are the seeds of wisdom." —Michael Singer, *The Untethered Soul*

From the Bible: "For Jehovah corrects the one he loves, just as a father does a son in whom he delights." —Proverbs 3:12

Reflection Question: What lesson did you learn from a difficult time this year, and how has it shaped your personal growth?

September 17th: Embracing Inner Strength

Inner strength is a valuable harvest. Today, reflect on the inner strength you've developed over the year.

Think about moments when you demonstrated resilience or courage. What inner resources did you draw upon? Write down your thoughts.

Recognize and celebrate your inner strength. Embrace the power within you to face future challenges with confidence.

Words of Wisdom: "You are stronger than you realize. Every difficulty reveals your true power." —Rhonda Byrne, *The Power*

From the Bible: "God is our refuge and strength, a help that is readily found in times of distress." —Psalm 46:1

Reflection Question: What inner strength have you discovered or developed this year, and how can you draw upon it in the future?

September 18th: Appreciating Spiritual Growth

Spiritual growth is a vital part of our inner harvest. Today, focus on the spiritual insights and connections you've gained this year.

Reflect on a spiritual practice or experience that deepened your faith or understanding. What did it teach you about yourself and the world? Write down your reflections.

Celebrate your spiritual growth and the peace it brings. Embrace the deeper connection you've cultivated with your higher self or the divine.

Words of Wisdom: "Spiritual growth is a journey of understanding your connection with the universe." —Dr. Joe Dispenza, *Becoming Supernatural*

From the Bible: "But grow in the undeserved kindness and knowledge of our Lord and Savior Jesus Christ." —2 Peter 3:18

Reflection Question: What spiritual growth have you experienced this year, and how has it enriched your life?

September 19th: Recognizing Emotional Growth

Emotional growth enhances our ability to navigate life's ups and downs. Today, reflect on how you've grown emotionally this year.

Think about a time when you managed your emotions effectively. What did you learn about yourself? Write down your thoughts.

Acknowledge the emotional maturity you've gained. Embrace the increased emotional intelligence that helps you relate better to yourself and others.

Words of Wisdom: "Emotional maturity is the ability to let go of what no longer serves us." —Pema Chodron, *Comfortable with Uncertainty*

From the Bible: "The one who is slow to anger has great discernment, but the impatient one displays his foolishness." —Proverbs 14:29

Reflection Question: What emotional growth have you experienced this year, and how has it impacted your relationships and well-being?

September 20th: Celebrating New Perspectives

New perspectives are part of our inner harvest. Today, reflect on how your perspectives have changed and broadened this year.

Think about a belief or opinion you've revised. What caused this shift? How has it affected your understanding of yourself and the world? Write down your reflections.

Celebrate the openness and growth that come from embracing new perspectives. Recognize the value of flexibility and curiosity in your personal development.

Words of Wisdom: "A shift in perspective can change your entire experience of life." —Oprah Winfrey

From the Bible: "He that is wise listens to advice." —Proverbs 12:15

Reflection Question: What new perspectives have you gained this year, and how have they contributed to your personal growth?

September 21st: Embracing Continuous Growth

Personal growth is an ongoing process. Today, focus on your commitment to continuous growth and development.

Reflect on the areas where you'd like to continue growing. What steps can you take to support your ongoing development? Write down your intentions.

Embrace the journey of continuous growth. Recognize that every step forward contributes to a richer, more fulfilling life.

Words of Wisdom: "Growth is a never-ending process of self-discovery." —Lynne McTaggart, *Living the Field*

From the Bible: "The righteous one may fall seven times, and he will get up again." —Proverbs 24:16

Reflection Question: What areas of your life are you committed to continuing to grow, and what steps will you take to support this growth?

Week 4: Grounding in Gratitude

Gratitude is a powerful practice that can transform our perspective and enhance our overall happiness and contentment. This week, we focus on grounding ourselves in gratitude, exploring various methods to cultivate a grateful heart. By consistently practicing gratitude, we can find joy in the present moment, appreciate the abundance in our lives, and foster a deep sense of fulfillment. Each day's devotion will offer practical ways to incorporate gratitude into your daily routine, drawing on wisdom from various spiritual and self-help sources.

September 22nd: Starting the Day with Gratitude

Beginning your day with gratitude sets a positive tone. Today, focus on starting your morning with a gratitude practice.

Upon waking, take a few moments to think about three things you are grateful for. They can be simple or significant. Write them down in a gratitude journal.

Notice how this practice shifts your mindset to a more positive and appreciative state. Embrace the sense of joy that comes from acknowledging your blessings first thing in the morning.

Words of Wisdom: "Begin each day with a heart full of gratitude, and you will see miracles unfold." —Rhonda Byrne, *The Power*

From the Bible: "Give thanks to Jehovah, for he is good; his loyal love endures forever." —Psalm 136:1

Reflection Question: What are three things you are grateful for this morning, and how does starting your day with gratitude affect your mood?

September 23rd: Practicing Mindful Gratitude

Mindfulness and gratitude go hand in hand. Today, focus on being mindful of the present moment and expressing gratitude for it.

Throughout your day, pause and take a deep breath. Notice your surroundings and identify something you appreciate in that moment. It could be the warmth of the sun, the sound of birds, or a kind gesture from someone.

Acknowledge these small moments of gratitude mindfully. Recognize how this practice enhances your awareness and appreciation of daily life.

Words of Wisdom: "Mindfulness combined with gratitude is a powerful force for inner peace." —Pema Chodron, *Comfortable with Uncertainty*

From the Bible: "Always rejoice in the Lord. I will say it again: Rejoice!" —Philippians 4:4

Reflection Question: How can you incorporate mindful gratitude into your day, and what effect does it have on your awareness and appreciation of the present moment?

September 24th: Gratitude Meditation

Meditation can deepen your sense of gratitude. Today, focus on a gratitude meditation practice.

Find a quiet place to sit comfortably. Close your eyes and take deep breaths. As you breathe, bring to mind things you are grateful for. Visualize them and feel the gratitude in your heart.

Spend a few minutes in this meditative state, allowing the feeling of gratitude to fill you. Notice how this practice brings peace and contentment.

Words of Wisdom: "Meditation on gratitude creates a bridge to a higher state of consciousness." —Dr. Joe Dispenza, *Becoming Supernatural*

From the Bible: "Let the peace of the Christ rule in your hearts, for you were, in fact, called to that peace in one body. And show yourselves thankful." —Colossians 3:15

Reflection Question: How does practicing gratitude meditation affect your sense of peace and contentment?

September 25th: Appreciation in Adversity

Embrace challenges as avenues for deep gratitude. Today, concentrate on uncovering the hidden thankfulness within tough circumstances.

Reflect on a recent challenge you encountered. What insights did you gain? How did it contribute to your personal growth? Record your thoughts.

Recognize the resilience and wisdom that come from overcoming challenges. See difficulties as opportunities for profound learning and self-improvement.

Words of Wisdom: "Adversity is an opportunity to find strength and gratitude in what remains." —Michael Singer, *The Untethered Soul*

From the Bible: "Even a fool is considered wise when he keeps silent, and discerning when he seals his lips." —Proverbs 17:28

Reflection Question: How can you find gratitude in a recent challenge, and what lessons or growth did it bring you?

September 26th: Expressing Celebrating Acts of Kindness

Today, shine a light on the kindness that others have shown you. This exercise is about recognizing those small gestures that often go unnoticed but significantly impact our lives.

Reflect on a recent act of kindness someone has extended towards you. It could be as simple as a supportive message during a tough time or someone sharing their time or resources.

In acknowledging these acts, you're not only fostering gratitude but also encouraging a culture of generosity and compassion. Celebrate these moments by reaching out to express your thanks or by paying it forward.

Words of Wisdom: "The ripple effect of kindness starts with gratitude." —Wayne Dyer, *There's a Spiritual Solution to Every Problem*

From the Bible: "Let us consider one another so as to incite to love and fine works." —Hebrews 10:24

Reflection Question: What recent act of kindness has touched your life, and how can you acknowledge or reciprocate it today?

September 27th: Gratitude for the Present Moment

Being grateful for the present moment can bring immense peace. Today, focus on appreciating where you are right now.

Reflect on your current situation and identify aspects you are grateful for. It could be the comfort of your home, your health, or the love of family and friends.

Embrace the present moment with gratitude. Recognize that even in imperfect circumstances, there is always something to be thankful for.

Words of Wisdom: "In the present moment, gratitude finds its purest form." —Pema Chodron, *Comfortable with Uncertainty*

From the Bible: "This is the day that Jehovah has made; let us rejoice and be glad in it." —Psalm 118:24

Reflection Question: What aspects of your current situation are you grateful for, and how does this gratitude bring you peace?

September 28th: Creating a Gratitude Ritual

Establishing a gratitude ritual can solidify the practice in your daily life. Today, focus on creating a consistent gratitude practice.

Choose a specific time each day to practice gratitude—morning, during meals, or before bed. Use a journal to write down three things you are grateful for each day.

Commit to this ritual and notice how it transforms your mindset over time. Embrace the habit of gratitude as a cornerstone of your daily routine.

Words of Wisdom: "Daily rituals of gratitude are the seeds for a fulfilling life." —Rhonda Byrne, *The Power*

From the Bible: "Continue in prayer, keeping awake in it with thanksgiving." —Colossians 4:2

Reflection Question: How can you incorporate a daily gratitude ritual into your life, and what changes do you notice as a result?

September 29th: Gratitude for Your Journey

Reflecting on your life's journey can bring a deep sense of gratitude. Today, focus on appreciating the path you've traveled, including the highs and lows.

Think about your life's journey—the experiences, lessons, and growth. Write down what you're grateful for from your past, and how these experiences have shaped who you are today.

Acknowledge the beauty in your unique journey. Embrace the gratitude for every step that has brought you to this moment.

Words of Wisdom: "The journey itself is the treasure, and gratitude is the map." —Michael Singer, *The Untethered Soul*

From the Bible: "The heart of man plans his way, but Jehovah establishes his steps." —Proverbs 16:9

Reflection Question: How has your life's journey shaped you, and what experiences are you most grateful for?

September 30th: Gratitude for Future Possibilities

Gratitude isn't just for the present and past—it's also for the future. Today, focus on being grateful for the possibilities that lie ahead.

Reflect on your hopes and dreams for the future. Write down what you're looking forward to and express gratitude for the opportunities that await you.

Embrace an optimistic and grateful outlook for the future. Recognize that gratitude can pave the way for new possibilities and experiences.

Words of Wisdom: "Gratitude for the future opens the door to unlimited possibilities." —Dr. Joe Dispenza, *Becoming Supernatural*

From the Bible: "For I well know the thoughts that I am thinking toward you, declares Jehovah, thoughts of peace and not of calamity, to give you a future and a hope." —Jeremiah 29:11

Reflection Question: What future possibilities are you grateful for, and how does this gratitude influence your outlook on life?

October: Embracing Transformation

October is a month of profound transformation, mirrored by the falling leaves and the preparation for winter. As trees shed their leaves, they remind us of the beauty in letting go and making way for new growth. This month, we focus on embracing personal transformation, recognizing that change, though sometimes challenging, can be powerful and renewing. Transformation allows us to shed old habits, thoughts, and patterns that no longer serve us, creating space for new possibilities and growth. Each day's devotion will guide you through this transformative process, encouraging you to embrace change with an open heart and a positive mindset, drawing on the wisdom of nature and spiritual insights. Let's embark on this journey of transformation together, finding strength and renewal in the process.

Week 1: Embracing Shadows with Compassion

We all have shadows—parts of ourselves that hold our fears, doubts, and challenges. Embracing these shadows with compassion is crucial for personal growth and transformation. This week, we will focus on confronting our shadows with understanding and kindness, recognizing that they are an integral part of our journey. By acknowledging and embracing our shadows, we can heal and integrate these aspects of ourselves, leading to greater wholeness and inner peace. Each day's devotion will provide guidance and reflections to help you navigate this process with grace and compassion.

October 1st: Acknowledging Your Shadows

The first step in embracing your shadows is to acknowledge their presence. Today, focus on identifying your fears, doubts, and challenges without judgment.

Think about an area of your life where you feel stuck or fearful. Write down the thoughts and emotions that come up when you reflect on this area.

Recognize that acknowledging your shadows is a brave and important step towards healing and transformation.

Words of Wisdom: "The wound is the place where the Light enters you." —Pema Chodron, *Comfortable with Uncertainty*

From the Bible: "For God gave us not a spirit of cowardice, but one of power and of love and of soundness of mind." —2 Timothy 1:7

Reflection Question: What shadows do you need to acknowledge today, and how can recognizing them help you move toward healing?

October 2nd: Understanding Your Shadows

Understanding your shadows involves exploring their origins and meanings. Today, focus on understanding the roots of your fears and challenges.

Reflect on a specific fear or doubt. Where did it originate? How has it affected your life? Write down your insights.

Approach this exploration with curiosity and compassion, recognizing that understanding your shadows can lead to deeper self-awareness and growth.

Words of Wisdom: "Understanding your darkness is the best method for dealing with the darknesses of other people." —Carl Jung, *A Course in Miracles*

From the Bible: "The light is shining in the darkness, and the darkness has not overpowered it." —John 1:5

Reflection Question: What have you learned about the origins of your shadows, and how does this understanding help you?

October 3rd: Embracing Self-Compassion

Self-compassion is essential when confronting your shadows. Today, focus on treating yourself with kindness and understanding as you navigate your inner challenges.

Think about a time when you were hard on yourself. How could you have approached that situation with more compassion? Write down your reflections.

Practice self-compassion today by speaking kindly to yourself and acknowledging your efforts and strengths.

Words of Wisdom: "Be kind to yourself as you proceed along this journey. Learn to love the person you are with." —Wayne Dyer, *There's a Spiritual Solution to Every Problem*

From the Bible: "Keep seeking peace and pursue it." —Psalm 34:14

Reflection Question: How can practicing self-compassion help you navigate your shadows and foster inner peace?

October 4th: Facing Fears with Courage

Facing your fears takes courage. Today, focus on confronting a fear with bravery and determination.

Identify a specific fear you want to address. What steps can you take to face it head-on? Write down a plan of action.

Take a small step today towards facing this fear. Recognize the courage it takes to confront your fears and celebrate your bravery.

When we face our fears with love, we discover that fear is not as powerful as love.

The only way to deal with fear is to face it head-on with love and understanding.

Words of Wisdom: "Fear is a natural reaction to moving closer to the truth." — Pema Chödrön

From the Bible: "Be courageous and strong. Do not be afraid or be terrified, for Jehovah your God is with you wherever you go." —Joshua 1:9

Reflection Question: What fear can you face with courage today, and what steps will you take to confront it?

October 5th: Transforming Doubts into Strengths

Doubts can be transformed into strengths through understanding and perseverance. Today, focus on transforming a specific doubt into a source of strength.

Reflect on a doubt that has held you back. How can you reframe this doubt as a challenge to overcome? Write down your thoughts.

Take a proactive step today to address this doubt and transform it into a strength. Recognize the inspiration that comes from this transformation.

Words of Wisdom: "Every doubt can be a stepping stone to greater strength and understanding." —Rhonda Byrne, *The Power*

From the Bible: "But those who hope in Jehovah will regain power. They will soar on wings like eagles. They will run and not grow weary; they will walk and not tire out." —Isaiah 40:31

Reflection Question: How can you transform a doubt into a strength today, and what actions will you take to make this transformation?

October 6th: Learning from Challenges

Challenges are valuable teachers. Today, focus on the lessons you can learn from a current or past challenge.

Think about a recent challenge you faced. What did it teach you about yourself, your strengths, and your areas for growth? Write down your reflections.

Embrace the lessons learned from challenges as opportunities for growth and development.

Words of Wisdom: "Difficulties come to instruct, not to obstruct." — Michael Singer, *The Untethered Soul*

From the Bible: "But the one who has endured to the end will be saved." —Matthew 24:13

Reflection Question: What lessons have you learned from a recent challenge, and how can you apply these lessons to your personal growth?

October 7th: Integrating Your Shadows

Integrating your shadows involves accepting them as part of your whole self. Today, focus on integrating your shadows with compassion and understanding.

Reflect on the shadows you've acknowledged this week. How can you accept and integrate these parts of yourself in a healthy and constructive way? Write down your thoughts.

Embrace your shadows as integral parts of your journey towards wholeness and self-acceptance.

Words of Wisdom: "To confront a person with his shadow is to show him his own light." —Carl Jung, *A Course in Miracles*

From the Bible: "Therefore, if anyone is in union with Christ, he is a new creation; the old things passed away, look! new things have come into existence." —2 Corinthians 5:17

Reflection Question: How can you integrate your shadows into your life with compassion, and what steps will you take to embrace your whole self?

Week 2: Nurturing Seeds of Transformation

Autumn is a season of preparation, much like gardeners planting bulbs that will bloom in spring. This week, we focus on nurturing seeds of transformation by setting new intentions that will lead to future growth. Just as nature prepares for renewal, we can plant the seeds of our desires and goals, allowing them to take root and flourish in time. Each day's devotion will guide you in identifying and nurturing these seeds of intention, drawing inspiration from spiritual teachings and wisdom from various self-help sources.

October 8th: Planting Seeds of Intention

Setting clear intentions is the first step towards transformation. Today, focus on identifying what you want to grow in your life.

Reflect on a specific goal or desire. Write down your intention clearly and concisely, as if planting a seed in fertile soil.

Visualize this seed taking root and growing. Trust that with care and attention, it will flourish in time.

Words of Wisdom: "Intention is the starting point of every dream." — Deepak Chopra

From the Bible: "Keep on asking, and it will be given you; keep on seeking, and you will find; keep on knocking, and it will be opened to you." —Matthew 7:7

Reflection Question: What seed of intention will you plant today, and how can you nurture its growth?

October 9th: Nurturing Your Intentions

Intentions, like seeds, need nurturing. Today, focus on the actions you can take to support the growth of your intentions.

Identify small, consistent actions that will help your intention take root. Write them down and commit to integrating them into your daily routine.

Recognize that nurturing your intentions requires patience and persistence. Celebrate each small step forward.

Words of Wisdom: "Growth takes time, and every small step is progress." —Wayne Dyer, *There's a Spiritual Solution to Every Problem*

From the Bible: "Commit to Jehovah whatever you do, and your plans will succeed." —Proverbs 16:3

Reflection Question: What actions can you take today to nurture your intentions, and how will you incorporate them into your routine?

October 10th: Visualizing Growth

Visualization is a powerful tool for manifesting your intentions. Today, focus on visualizing the growth and fruition of your intentions.

Find a quiet place to sit comfortably. Close your eyes and visualize your intention as a fully grown plant. See it flourishing and bearing fruit.

Feel the emotions associated with this vision—joy, fulfillment, peace. Let these feelings reinforce your commitment to nurturing your intention.

Words of Wisdom: "See it in your mind's eye, and it will manifest in your life." —Rhonda Byrne, *The Power*

From the Bible: "Now faith is the assured expectation of what is hoped for, the evident demonstration of realities that are not seen." —Hebrews 11:1

Reflection Question: How can visualization help you nurture your intentions, and what does your fully grown intention look like?

October 11th: Trusting the Process

Trust is essential when nurturing new growth. Today, focus on trusting the process and having faith in the natural progression of your intentions.

Reflect on past experiences where patience and trust led to positive outcomes. Write down how trust played a role in these experiences.

Affirm your faith in the process of growth. Recognize that each stage is necessary and valuable.

Words of Wisdom: "Trust the process. Your time is coming." — Sadhguru, *Inner Engineering*

From the Bible: "Commit to Jehovah whatever you do, and your plans will succeed." —Proverbs 16:3

Reflection Question: How can you cultivate trust in the process of nurturing your intentions, and what past experiences remind you of the importance of trust?

October 12th: Learning from Nature

Nature offers valuable lessons in growth and transformation. Today, focus on observing nature and applying its wisdom to your own life.

Spend time outdoors observing plants, trees, and the changing seasons. Reflect on how nature patiently grows and adapts.

Write down any insights you gain from this observation. Consider how you can apply these natural principles to nurturing your intentions.

Words of Wisdom: "Nature does not hurry, yet everything is accomplished." —Lao Tzu

From the Bible: "For everything there is an appointed time, even a time for every affair under the heavens." —Ecclesiastes 3:1

Reflection Question: What lessons from nature can you apply to nurturing your intentions, and how can observing nature inspire your growth?

October 13th: Removing Obstacles

Removing obstacles is crucial for growth. Today, focus on identifying and addressing anything that hinders your intentions.

Think about potential obstacles—doubts, fears, external barriers. Write down each obstacle and possible ways to overcome them.

Take a proactive step today to remove or mitigate one obstacle. Recognize the power of clearing the path for growth.

Words of Wisdom: "You may not see it now, but God is working behind scenes. He's lining up what you need, removing the wrong people and arranging things in your favor. Stay in faith." —Joel Osteen

From the Bible: "For God is my refuge, the God who shows loyal love to me." —Psalm 59:17

Reflection Question: What obstacles are hindering your intentions, and what steps can you take today to remove or overcome them?

October 14th: Celebrating Small Wins

Small wins are milestones in the journey of growth. Today, focus on celebrating the progress you've made in nurturing your intentions.

Reflect on the steps you've taken so far. Write down your achievements, no matter how small they may seem.

Celebrate these wins with gratitude and joy. Recognize that each step forward is a valuable part of your transformation.

Words of Wisdom: "Success is built on small victories." —Rhonda Byrne, *The Power*

From the Bible: "Do not despise these small beginnings, for Jehovah rejoices to see the work begin." —Zechariah 4:10

Reflection Question: What small wins can you celebrate today, and how do they contribute to your overall growth and transformation?

Week 3: Aligning with Inner Balance

Finding balance in our lives is essential for overall well-being and happiness. This week, we focus on aligning our personal, professional, and spiritual selves to create harmony and peace. Balancing these aspects of our lives allows us to feel more centered and fulfilled. Each day's devotion will offer practical tips and fun activities to help you harmonize different areas of your life, making it easier to navigate your day with a sense of equilibrium and joy.

October 15th: Balancing Work and Play

Balancing work and play are crucial for maintaining energy and joy. Today, focus on incorporating fun activities into your schedule.

Plan a fun activity to do after work, such as a hobby you enjoy, a walk in the park, or a movie night. Make sure it's something that brings you joy and relaxation.

Notice how taking time to play enhances your productivity and mood. Embrace the balance between work and leisure.

Words of Wisdom: "You can discover more about a person in an hour of play than in a year of conversation." —Plato

From the Bible: "There is nothing better for a man than to eat and drink and find enjoyment in his hard work. This too, I have realized, is from the hand of the true God." —Ecclesiastes 2:24

Reflection Question: How can you balance work and play today to enhance your well-being?

October 16th: Creating a Morning Routine

A balanced morning routine sets a positive tone for the day. Today, focus on creating a morning routine that nurtures your personal, professional, and spiritual selves.

Start your day with a few minutes of meditation or prayer, followed by a healthy breakfast and some light exercise. Plan your day with intention, prioritizing tasks that align with your goals.

Notice how a balanced morning routine helps you feel more focused and energized throughout the day.

Words of Wisdom: "The way you start your day can determine how well you live your day." —Wayne Dyer, *There's a Spiritual Solution to Every Problem*

From the Bible: "In the morning, O Jehovah, you will hear my voice; in the morning I will express my concern to you and wait expectantly." —Psalm 5:3

Reflection Question: What elements can you include in your morning routine to create balance and start your day positively?

October 17th: Integrating Mindfulness into Your Day

Mindfulness helps maintain balance by keeping you present. Today, focus on integrating mindfulness into your daily activities.

Choose an activity, like eating lunch or walking, and do it mindfully. Pay full attention to the experience, noticing the details and sensations.

Notice how mindfulness helps you stay centered and reduces stress. Embrace the balance that comes from being fully present.

Words of Wisdom: "Mindfulness is the key to being fully alive." — Thich Nhat Hanh

From the Bible: "Do not be anxious about anything, but in everything by prayer and supplication along with thanksgiving, let your petitions be made known to God." —Philippians 4:6

Reflection Question: How can you integrate mindfulness into your daily activities to enhance balance and presence?

October 18th: Balancing Social Time and Solitude

Both social time and solitude are important for balance. Today, focus on finding a healthy mix of both.·

Schedule time to connect with friends or family, and also set aside time for yourself. Enjoy a social activity and later indulge in some quiet time to read, meditate, or simply relax.

Notice how balancing social interactions with alone time helps you feel more refreshed and content.

Words of Wisdom: "A little while alone in your room will prove more valuable than anything else that could ever be given you." —Rumi

From the Bible: "But when you pray, go into your private room, and after shutting your door, pray to your Father who is in secret. Then your Father who looks on in secret will repay you." — Matthew 6:6.

Reflection Question: How can you balance social activities with solitude today to nurture your personal well-being?

October 19th: Prioritizing Self-Care

Self-care is essential for maintaining balance. Today, focus on prioritizing self-care activities that rejuvenate you.

Schedule a self-care activity, such as a relaxing bath, a massage, or reading a good book. Make it a priority and treat it as an important appointment.

Notice how taking time for self-care enhances your overall mood and productivity. Embrace the balance that self-care brings to your life.

Words of Wisdom: "Let yourself be silently drawn by the strange pull of what you really love. It will not lead you astray." —Rumi

From the Bible: "Come to me, all you who are toiling and loaded down, and I will refresh you." —Matthew 11:28

Reflection Question: What self-care activity can you prioritize today to nurture your well-being?

October 20th: Balancing Technology Use

Technology can both connect and overwhelm us. Today, focus on balancing your use of technology.

Set specific times for checking emails and social media, and designate tech-free times for reading, exercising, or spending time with loved ones. Notice how this balance affects your stress levels and mood.

Embrace the balance that comes from mindful technology use, and enjoy the increased focus and presence it brings.

Words of Wisdom: "It has become appallingly obvious that our Technology has exceeded our humanity." —Albert Einstein

From the Bible: "Better is a handful of rest than two handfuls of hard work and chasing after the wind." —Ecclesiastes 4:6

Reflection Question: How can you balance technology use today to enhance your focus and presence?

October 21st: Balancing Giving and Receiving

Both giving and receiving are important for balance. Today, focus on finding harmony between these two aspects.

Perform an act of kindness for someone, and also allow yourself to receive help or kindness from others. Notice how both giving and receiving contribute to a sense of balance and connection.

Recognize the importance of this reciprocity in maintaining healthy relationships and personal well-being.

Words of Wisdom: "The more you give, the more you receive." — Wayne Dyer, *There's a Spiritual Solution to Every Problem*

From the Bible: "There is more happiness in giving than there is in receiving." —Acts 20:35

Reflection Question: How can you balance giving and receiving today to foster a sense of connection and well-being?

Week 4: Embracing the Beauty of Impermanence

Autumn's changing colors beautifully illustrate the impermanence of life. The vibrant leaves that transform and eventually fall remind us that change is a natural part of existence. This week, we focus on embracing the beauty of impermanence, learning to appreciate the transient moments in life. By understanding and accepting that everything is temporary, we can find joy and beauty in the present moment. Each day's devotion will guide you in reflecting on the lessons of impermanence and how they can enhance your appreciation of life's fleeting moments.

October 22nd: Appreciating Fleeting Moments

Life's fleeting moments are precious. Today, focus on appreciating the transient beauty around you.

Spend a few minutes observing the changing leaves, the sunset, or a blooming flower. Take in the beauty of these temporary moments.

Reflect on how the impermanence of these moments makes them even more special. Embrace the present with a sense of wonder and gratitude.

Words of Wisdom: "Yesterday I was clever, so it wanted to change the world. Today I am wise, so I am changing myself." —Rumi

From the Bible: "This is the day that Jehovah has made; let us rejoice and be joyful in it." —Psalm 118:24

Reflection Question: What fleeting moments can you appreciate today, and how does their impermanence enhance their beauty?

October 23rd: Finding Joy in Change

Change brings new beauty and opportunities. Today, focus on finding joy in the changes happening around you.

Identify a recent change in your life. Reflect on the new opportunities and experiences it has brought. Write down what you appreciate about this change.

Embrace the joy that comes from change, recognizing that it brings growth and new perspectives.

Words of Wisdom: "Change the way you look at things and the things you look at will change." —Wayne Dyer

From the Bible: "And the one seated on the throne said: 'Look! I am making all things new.'" —Revelation 21:5

Reflection Question: What recent changes can you find joy in, and how have they brought new opportunities into your life?

October 24th: Letting Go with Grace

Letting go is a natural part of embracing impermanence. Today, focus on letting go of something with grace.

Think about something you need to let go of—an old habit, a past regret, or a limiting belief. Reflect on how releasing it can make space for new growth.

Embrace the freedom that comes from letting go, trusting that it is a step towards renewal.

Words of Wisdom: "To let go is to release the grip of fear and welcome the freedom of growth." —Pema Chodron, *Comfortable with Uncertainty*

From the Bible: "Do not be anxious about anything." —Philippians 4:6

Reflection Question: What can you let go of today, and how does letting go create space for new growth?

October 25th: Embracing New Beginnings

Every ending is a new beginning. Today, focus on embracing the new beginnings that come from endings.

Reflect on a recent ending in your life—a job, a relationship, a phase. What new beginnings has it brought? Write down your reflections.

Celebrate the opportunities that new beginnings offer. Embrace them with an open heart and an adventurous spirit.

Words of Wisdom: "The beginning is the most important part of the work." —Plato

From the Bible: "And I will put a new spirit within you." —Ezekiel 36:26

Reflection Question: What new beginnings can you embrace today, and how do they bring excitement and growth into your life?

October 26th: Living Fully in the Present

Impermanence teaches us to live fully in the present. Today, focus on being fully present in your activities.

Choose an activity you often rush through—eating, walking, talking. Slow down and fully engage in the experience.

Notice how being present enhances your enjoyment and appreciation of the moment. Embrace the fullness of now.

Words of Wisdom: "Living in the present moment creates the experience of eternity." —Eckhart Tolle -The Power is Now.

From the Bible: "Satisfy us with your loyal love in the morning, so that we may shout joyfully and rejoice during all our days." — Psalms 90:14.

Reflection Question: How can you be more present today, and how does living fully in the present enhance your experience?

October 27th: Embracing the Cycle of Life

Life's cycles are a testament to impermanence. Today, focus on embracing the natural cycles of life.

Reflect on the cycles in your own life—birth, growth, decay, and renewal. Write down how these cycles have shaped your experiences and growth.

Recognize the beauty and continuity in life's cycles. Embrace the wisdom they offer.

Words of Wisdom: "All life is cyclic; it is the law of change." — Sadhguru, *Inner Engineering*

From the Bible: "There is a time to weep and a time to laugh; a time to mourn and a time to dance." —Ecclesiastes 3:4

Reflection Question: How can you embrace the natural cycles in your life, and what wisdom do they offer you?

October 28th: Appreciating Life's Fragility

Life's fragility reminds us to cherish each moment. Today, focus on appreciating the fragile beauty of life.

Reflect on a precious moment or a loved one. Write down what makes them special and how you can cherish them more.

Embrace the preciousness of life, recognizing that its fragility makes it even more valuable.

Words of Wisdom: "The fragility of life is what makes it so beautiful." —Rhonda Byrne, *The Power*

From the Bible: "Teach us to count our days so that we may acquire a heart of wisdom." —Psalm 90:12

Reflection Question: What or who can you cherish more today, and how does appreciating life's fragility enhance your gratitude?

October 29th: Finding Peace in Change

Change can bring peace when we accept it. Today, focus on finding peace in the changes happening in your life.

Reflect on a change you're currently experiencing. How can you find peace in this transition? Write down your thoughts.

Embrace the serenity that comes from accepting change. Trust that each change is part of a larger plan.

Words of Wisdom: "True peace comes from embracing change." — Michael Singer, *The Untethered Soul*

From the Bible: "Peace I leave with you; my peace I give to you." — John 14:27

Reflection Question: How can you find peace in a current change, and what steps can you take to embrace this transition with serenity?

October 30th: Gratitude for Impermanence

Impermanence makes gratitude possible. Today, focus on being grateful for the temporary nature of life's moments.

Think about a beautiful moment that has passed. Reflect on the joy it brought you and write down why you're grateful for that experience.

Recognize that impermanence enhances the value of these moments. Embrace gratitude for the transient beauty of life.

Words of Wisdom: "Impermanence is what makes every moment so precious." —Pema Chodron, *Comfortable with Uncertainty*

From the Bible: "For just as the rain and the snow pour down from heaven and do not return there until they have saturated the earth, making it produce and sprout, giving seed to the sower and bread to the eater, so my word that goes out of my mouth will be. It will not return to me without results, but it will certainly accomplish whatever is my delight, and it will have sure success in what I send it to do." —Isaiah 55:10-11

Reflection Question: What past moment are you grateful for today, and how does its impermanence make it more precious?

October 31st: Embracing Life's Flow

Life's flow is ever-changing. Today, focus on embracing the natural flow of life with acceptance and grace.

Reflect on how life's flow has brought you to where you are now. Write down the events and changes that have shaped your path.

Embrace the flow of life, trusting that it will continue to guide you toward growth and fulfillment.

Words of Wisdom: "Life flows like a river; you can either ride the current or struggle against it." —Sadhguru, *Engineering*

From the Bible: "The name of Jehovah is a strong tower. The righteous run into it and are protected." —Proverbs 18:10

Reflection Question: How can you embrace the flow of life today, and what steps will you take to move forward with grace and acceptance?

November: Cultivating Inner Warmth

As the external world cools and winter approaches, it's essential to focus on cultivating inner warmth. November invites us to generate warmth from within through acts of kindness, meaningful connections, and caring for others. By fostering a warm and compassionate heart, we can navigate the colder months with a sense of inner peace and fulfillment. This month, we will explore various ways to create and sustain this inner warmth, drawing on the power of love, generosity, and connection. Each day's devotion will guide you in nurturing these qualities, ensuring that your inner light continues to shine brightly, even as the days grow shorter and colder. Embrace the opportunity to radiate warmth to yourself and those around you, finding joy in the simple, heartfelt moments of kindness and care.

Week 1: Embracing the Spirit of Gratitude

Gratitude has the power to warm our hearts and strengthen our connections with others. This week, we focus on embracing and expressing gratitude, recognizing its ability to bring warmth and joy into our lives and the lives of those around us. By cultivating a spirit of thankfulness, we can enhance our sense of well-being and deepen our relationships. Each day's devotion will guide you in finding ways to practice and express gratitude, making it a cornerstone of your daily life. Let's embark on this journey of thankfulness, spreading warmth and kindness through our heartfelt appreciation.

November 1st: Cultivating Warmth through Kindness

As the temperatures drop, let the warmth within you rise through acts of kindness. Today, focus on how small gestures can create significant warmth in the hearts of others.

Perform a simple act of kindness, such as holding the door for someone, paying a compliment, or helping a neighbor with a task. Notice how these small actions not only brighten someone else's day but also fill you with a sense of warmth and connection.

Kindness has a ripple effect, spreading warmth far beyond the initial act. Embrace the power of these small, thoughtful gestures to make a big difference.

Words of Wisdom: "The simplest acts of kindness are by far more powerful than a thousand heads bowing in prayer." —Mahatma Gandhi

From the Bible: "But the fruitage of the spirit is love, joy, peace, patience, kindness, goodness, faith." —Galatians 5:22

Reflection Question: What small act of kindness can you perform today, and how does it make you feel?

November 2nd: Expressing Gratitude to Others

Expressing gratitude to others strengthens relationships. Today, focus on sharing your appreciation with someone important to you.

Think of someone who has made a positive impact on your life. Write them a heartfelt note or tell them in person why you appreciate them.

Notice the positive energy that flows from expressing gratitude. Recognize how this practice enhances your connections and spreads joy.

Words of Wisdom: "Gratitude is not only the greatest of virtues but the parent of all others." —Cicero

From the Bible: "Therefore encourage one another and build one another up, just as you are doing." —1 Thessalonians 5:11

Reflection Question: Who can you express gratitude to today, and how does this act of appreciation strengthen your relationship?

November 3rd: Gratitude for Challenges

Even challenges offer opportunities for gratitude. Today, focus on finding gratitude in difficult situations.

Think about a recent challenge you faced. What did you learn from it? How did it help you grow? Write down your reflections.

Acknowledge the growth and strength gained from facing challenges. Embrace the perspective that difficulties can be valuable teachers.

Words of Wisdom: "Obstacles are great incentives." —Pema Chodron, *Comfortable with Uncertainty*

From the Bible: "Let perseverance finish its work so that you may be mature and complete, not lacking anything." —James 1:4

Reflection Question: How has a recent challenge enriched your life or altered your perspective on adversity?

November 4th: Gratitude for Simple Joys

Simple joys often bring the most warmth to our hearts. Today, focus on being grateful for the simple pleasures in life.

Take a moment to enjoy a simple joy, like a warm cup of tea, a walk in nature, or a cozy blanket. Reflect on the comfort and happiness these simple things bring.

Notice how appreciating simple joys can fill your heart with warmth and contentment.

Words of Wisdom: "Happiness consists not in things, but in the relish we have of them." —Michel de Montaigne

From the Bible: "This is the day that Jehovah has made; let us rejoice and be joyful in it." —Psalm 118:24

Reflection Question: What simple joys can you appreciate today, and how do they bring warmth to your heart?

November 5th: Gratitude for Loved Ones

Our loved ones are a source of warmth and joy. Today, focus on expressing gratitude for the people who enrich your life.

Think about the people you are grateful for. Reach out to them with a call, message, or hug, and let them know how much they mean to you.

Recognize the love and support your loved ones provide. Embrace the warmth that comes from these cherished connections.

Words of Wisdom: "A loving heart is the truest wisdom." —Charles Dickens

From the Bible: "Dear friends, let us love one another, because love is from God, and everyone who loves has been born from God and knows God." —1 John 4:7

Reflection Question: Who are you grateful for today, and how can you show your appreciation for them?

November 6th: Gratitude for Health

Good health is a precious gift. Today, focus on expressing gratitude for your health and well-being.

Reflect on the aspects of your health you are grateful for, whether it's physical, mental, or emotional well-being. Write down your thoughts.

Appreciate the strength and vitality your health provides. Embrace the commitment to taking care of your body and mind.

Words of Wisdom: "To keep the body in good health is a duty... otherwise we shall not be able to keep our mind strong and clear." — Buddha

From the Bible: "Beloved, I pray that you may prosper in all respects and that you may be in good health, just as your soul is prospering." — 3 John 1:2

Reflection Question: What aspects of your health are you grateful for today, and how can you nurture and maintain them?

November 7th: Gratitude for New Opportunities

New opportunities bring growth and excitement. Today, focus on being grateful for the opportunities that come your way.

Think about a recent opportunity you received. Reflect on how it has positively impacted your life and write down your gratitude.

Embrace the excitement and possibilities that new opportunities bring. Recognize the abundance in your life.

Words of Wisdom: "Opportunities are like sunrises. If you wait too long, you miss them." —William Arthur Ward

From the Bible: "See, I have set before you an opened door, which no one can shut." —Revelation 3:8

Reflection Question: What new opportunities are you grateful for today, and how can you make the most of them?

Week 2: Connecting with Inner Peace

As the year winds down, it's a perfect time to connect with inner peace. This week, we will explore various practices that help us find tranquility amidst the busyness of life. Whether through meditation, prayer, or quiet contemplation, these practices allow us to center ourselves and cultivate a sense of calm. By prioritizing moments of stillness, we can navigate the end of the year with grace and serenity. Each day's devotion will offer practical ways to incorporate these peaceful practices into your daily routine, helping you find balance and inner harmony.

November 8th: Meditation for Inner Peace

Meditation is a powerful tool for cultivating inner peace. Today, focus on incorporating a short meditation into your routine.

Find a quiet place to sit comfortably. Close your eyes and take deep breaths. Focus on your breath, letting go of any tension or stress.

Spend at least five minutes in this meditative state, allowing your mind to settle and your heart to find peace.

Words of Wisdom: "Meditation is not a means to an end. It is both the means and the end." —Jiddu Krishnamurti

From the Bible: "Be still, and know that I am God." —Psalm 46:10

Reflection Question: How can you incorporate a short meditation into your daily routine, and what benefits do you notice from this practice?

November 9th: The Power of Prayer

Prayer is a deeply personal way to connect with inner peace. Today, focus on spending time in prayer, seeking comfort and guidance.

Find a quiet space where you can pray without distractions. Speak from your heart, sharing your thoughts, concerns, and gratitude with God.

Notice the sense of peace that comes from entrusting your worries and joys to a higher power.

Words of Wisdom: "Prayer is not asking. It is a longing of the soul." — Mahatma Gandhi

From the Bible: "Do not be anxious over anything, but in everything by prayer and supplication along with thanksgiving, let your petitions be made known to God." —Philippians 4:6

Reflection Question: How does prayer help you connect with inner peace, and how can you make time for it each day?

November 10th: Quiet Contemplation

Quiet contemplation allows us to reflect and find stillness. Today, focus on setting aside time for quiet contemplation.

Choose a peaceful spot, perhaps in nature or a cozy corner of your home. Sit quietly and let your mind wander, reflecting on your day, your goals, and your blessings.

Embrace the tranquility that comes from this practice, allowing your thoughts to flow without judgment.

Words of Wisdom: "In quietness and in confidence shall be your strength." —Isaiah 30:15

From the Bible: "The Lord is good to those who hope in him, to the one seeking him." —Lamentations 3:25

Reflection Question: How can quiet contemplation bring peace to your day, and what insights do you gain from this practice?

November 11th: Journaling for Peace

Journaling can be a therapeutic way to connect with inner peace. Today, focus on writing down your thoughts and feelings.

Take some time to write in a journal. Reflect on your day, your emotions, and any challenges or victories you experienced. Use this time to process and release any tension.

Notice how putting your thoughts on paper can bring clarity and calm.

Words of Wisdom: "Writing in a journal reminds you of your goals and of your learning in life. It offers a place where you can hold a deliberate, thoughtful conversation with yourself." —Robin Sharma

From the Bible: "A man's steps are established by Jehovah; and he takes pleasure in his way." —Psalm 37:23

Reflection Question: How does journaling help you connect with inner peace, and what benefits do you notice from this practice?

November 12th: Connecting with Nature

Nature has a calming effect on the soul. Today, focus on spending time outdoors to connect with inner peace.

Take a walk in a park, hike a trail, or simply sit in your backyard. Pay attention to the sights, sounds, and smells around you. Let nature's beauty and tranquility wash over you.

Feel the peace that comes from being in nature and appreciate the simple joys it offers.

Words of Wisdom: "Nature is the best medicine for serenity. Peace, calmness, stillness. It's good for the heart." —Karen Madwell

From the Bible: "For his invisible qualities are clearly seen from the world's creation onward, because they are perceived by the things made." —Romans 1:20

Reflection Question: How does spending time in nature help you find inner peace, and how can you make this a regular practice?

November 13th: Mindful Breathing

Mindful breathing is a simple yet effective way to center yourself. Today, focus on using mindful breathing to find peace.

Whenever you feel stressed or overwhelmed, take a moment to breathe deeply. Inhale slowly through your nose, hold for a few seconds, and exhale through your mouth. Repeat this several times.

Notice how mindful breathing calms your mind and relaxes your body, helping you return to a state of peace.

Words of Wisdom: "Feelings come and go like clouds in a windy sky. Conscious breathing is my anchor." —Thich Nhat Hanh

From the Bible: "For the spirit of God has made me, and the breath of the Almighty gives me life." —Job 33:4

Reflection Question: How can mindful breathing help you manage stress and connect with inner peace, and when can you practice this throughout your day?

November 14th: Gratitude Meditation

Combining gratitude with meditation enhances its calming effects. Today, focus on a gratitude meditation to cultivate peace.

Find a quiet place to sit comfortably. Close your eyes and take deep breaths. Think of three things you are grateful for and visualize them in your mind. Feel the gratitude fill your heart.

Spend a few minutes in this state of gratitude, noticing how it brings warmth and peace.

Words of Wisdom: "Gratitude is the fairest blossom which springs from the soul." —Henry Ward Beecher

From the Bible: "Enter his gates with thanksgiving and his courtyards with praise. Give thanks to him; bless his name." —Psalm 100:4

Reflection Question: How does practicing gratitude meditation help you connect with inner peace, and how can you make this a regular part of your routine?

Week 3: Embracing Self-Compassion

Self-compassion is about treating ourselves with the same kindness and understanding that we would offer to a dear friend. This week, we will explore the theme of self-compassion, learning how to be gentle with ourselves and embrace our imperfections. By practicing self-compassion, we can build resilience, improve our mental health, and foster a more loving relationship with ourselves. Each day's devotion will provide practical strategies and insights to help you nurture self-compassion in your daily life. Let's embark on this journey together, cultivating a compassionate heart towards ourselves.

November 15th: Valuing Personal Growth

Today, shift your focus from inherent worth to valuing your personal growth and the learning journey. Recognize how your past challenges and experiences have contributed to who you are today, reinforcing your self-compassion.

Reflect on the lessons learned from both successes and setbacks. Write down three key experiences that have shaped your personal growth. Consider how these have enhanced your resilience, wisdom, or empathy towards yourself and others.

Incorporate a mindfulness practice focusing on personal growth. As you encounter challenges or reflections throughout the day, take a moment to acknowledge how they contribute to your ongoing development.

Words of Wisdom: "Growth is not linear. It's a journey with twists and turns." —Michael Singer, *The Untethered Soul*

From the Bible: "And we know that all things work together for good to those who love God." —Romans 8:28

Reflection Question: What are three key growth experiences in your life, and how have these influenced your self-compassion and personal development?

November 16th: Speaking Kindly to Yourself

The way we speak to ourselves can greatly impact our self-compassion. Today, focus on using kind and encouraging words when you talk to yourself.

Pay attention to your inner dialogue. If you notice any self-critical thoughts, gently replace them with supportive and loving words. Treat yourself as you would a close friend.

Notice the shift in your mood and self-perception when you speak kindly to yourself. Embrace the power of positive self-talk.

Words of Wisdom: "You yourself, as much as anybody in the entire universe, deserve your love and affection." —Buddha

From the Bible: "A word spoken at the right time—how good it is!" —Proverbs 15:23

Reflection Question: How can you speak kindlier to yourself today, and what positive affirmations can you use to encourage yourself?

November 17th: Forgiving Yourself

Forgiveness is a vital part of self-compassion. Today, focus on forgiving yourself for past mistakes and embracing your humanity.

Think about a mistake or regret you've been holding onto. Write a letter to yourself, expressing understanding and forgiveness. Acknowledge that everyone makes mistakes and that it's a part of being human.

Notice the relief that comes from forgiving yourself. Embrace the freedom that self-forgiveness brings.

Words of Wisdom: "Forgive yourself for not knowing what you didn't know before you learned it." —Maya Angelou

From the Bible: "But you, O man of God, flee from these things, and pursue righteousness, godliness, faith, love, endurance, and mildness." —1 Timothy 6:11

Reflection Question: What mistake or regret can you forgive yourself for today, and how does self-forgiveness help you move forward?

November 18th: Taking Care of Your Body

Self-compassion includes taking care of your physical well-being. Today, focus on nurturing your body with kindness and care.

Plan a self-care activity that promotes your health, such as a gentle workout, a nutritious meal, or a relaxing bath. Treat your body with the respect and love it deserves.

Notice how taking care of your body enhances your overall well-being. Embrace the practice of physical self-care as a form of compassion.

Words of Wisdom: "Nourishing yourself in a way that helps you blossom in the direction you want to go is attainable, and you are worth the effort." —Deborah Day

From the Bible: "Do you not know that you yourselves are God's temple and that the spirit of God dwells in you?" —1 Corinthians 3:16

Reflection Question: How can you take better care of your body today, and what self-care activities can you incorporate into your routine?

November 19th: Allowing Yourself to Rest

Rest is an essential aspect of self-compassion. Today, focus on allowing yourself to rest and recharge.

Schedule some downtime to relax and do nothing. Whether it's a nap, reading a book, or simply sitting quietly, give yourself permission to rest without guilt.

Notice the rejuvenation that comes from resting. Embrace rest as a necessary part of self-care and compassion.

Words of Wisdom: "To be yourself in a world that is constantly trying to make you something else is the greatest accomplishment." —Ralph Waldo Emerson

From the Bible: "For we all stumble many times. If anyone does not stumble in word, he is a perfect man, able to bridle also his whole body." —James 3:2

Reflection Question: How can you incorporate more rest into your life, and how does allowing yourself to rest benefit your overall well-being?

November 20th: Accepting Your Imperfections

Self-compassion involves accepting your imperfections. Today, focus on embracing your flaws and understanding that they make you unique.

Think about an imperfection or flaw that you struggle with. Reflect on how it contributes to your uniqueness and growth. Write down ways in which you can view this imperfection with compassion.

Notice the relief that comes from accepting your imperfections. Embrace the beauty of your uniqueness.

Words of Wisdom: "To be yourself in a world that is constantly trying to make you something else is the greatest accomplishment" - Ralph Waldo Emerson

From the Bible: "For we all stumble many times. If anyone does not stumble in word, this one is a perfect man, able to bridle the whole body also." —James 3:2

Reflection Question: How can you view your imperfections with compassion, and what steps can you take to embrace them?

November 21st: Celebrating Small Victories

Recognizing and celebrating your achievements, no matter how small, is an act of self-compassion. Today, focus on acknowledging your progress.

Reflect on a recent accomplishment or positive change in your life. Celebrate this victory by treating yourself to something you enjoy or simply acknowledging it with gratitude.

Notice how celebrating small victories boosts your self-esteem and motivation. Embrace the practice of recognizing and honoring your progress.

Words of Wisdom: "Success is not final; failure is not fatal; it is the courage to continue that counts." —Winston Churchill

From the Bible: "Rejoice in the Lord always. Again, I will say, Rejoice!" —Philippians 4:4

Reflection Question: What recent accomplishment can you celebrate today, and how does acknowledging your progress enhance your self-compassion?

Week 4: Radiating Love and Kindness

Radiating love and kindness outward is a powerful way to create positive change in the world around us. This week, we focus on extending our compassion and generosity to others, recognizing that even small acts of kindness can have a significant impact. By spreading love and kindness, we not only uplift those around us but also experience the joy and fulfillment that comes from giving. Each day's devotion will provide practical ways to share kindness and love, encouraging you to make a difference in your community. Let's embrace the ripple effect of our actions, knowing that the love we give returns to us tenfold.

November 22nd: The Power of a Smile

A simple smile can brighten someone's day. Today, focus on sharing your smile with others.

Smile at people you encounter throughout your day—family, friends, coworkers, or even strangers. Notice how this small act of kindness can lift their spirits and yours.

Recognize the warmth and connection that a genuine smile can create. Embrace the power of this simple gesture to spread joy.

Words of Wisdom: "A smile is a curve that sets everything straight." — Phyllis Diller

From the Bible: "A joyful heart makes a cheerful face, but with a heartache comes depression." —Proverbs 15:13

Reflection Question: How can you use your smile to spread kindness today, and what impact does it have on your interactions?

November 23rd: Acts of Generosity

Generosity, big or small, makes a difference. Today, focus on performing acts of generosity.

Think of a way you can be generous today, whether it's buying someone a coffee, donating to a cause, or helping a neighbor. Take action and notice the positive effects.

Feel the joy and fulfillment that comes from giving. Embrace the ripple effect of your generosity.

Words of Wisdom: "You have not lived today until you have done something for someone who can never repay you." —John Bunyan

From the Bible: "There is more happiness in giving than there is in receiving." —Acts 20:35

Reflection Question: What act of generosity can you perform today, and how does it make you feel?

November 24th: Listening with Compassion

Listening with compassion can make others feel valued and understood. Today, focus on being a compassionate listener.

Engage in a conversation with someone, giving them your full attention. Listen without interrupting, and show empathy and understanding.

Notice how your compassionate listening strengthens your connection with others. Embrace the impact of being truly present.

Words of Wisdom: "Deep listening is the kind of listening that can help relieve the suffering of another person." —Thich Nhat Hanh

From the Bible: "My beloved brothers, be swift about hearing, slow about speaking, slow about wrath." —James 1:19

Reflection Question: How can you practice compassionate listening today, and what difference does it make in your relationships?

November 25th: Offering a Helping Hand

Helping others is a tangible way to show kindness. Today, focus on offering a helping hand to someone in need.

Look for opportunities to assist someone, whether it's carrying groceries, offering a ride, or providing emotional support. Act with kindness and willingness.

Notice the gratitude and connection that comes from helping others. Embrace the fulfillment of being a source of support.

Words of Wisdom: "When you give of yourself to others, you uncover the deepest parts of your soul, where love and purpose reside." —Pema Chodron, *Comfortable with Uncertainty*

From the Bible: "Carry one another's burdens, and so fulfill the law of Christ." —Galatians 6:2

Reflection Question: Who can you help today, and how does offering a helping hand enrich your own life?

November 26th: Sharing Kind Words

Kind words can uplift and encourage. Today, focus on sharing kind words with those around you.

Compliment someone sincerely, offer words of encouragement, or simply express your appreciation. Notice the positive reaction and connection that kind words create.

Recognize the power of your words to spread love and positivity. Embrace the habit of speaking kindly.

Words of Wisdom: "One kind word can warm three winter months." —Japanese Proverb

From the Bible: "The tongue of the wise makes knowledge appealing, but the mouth of the fool blurts out foolishness." —Proverbs 15:2

Reflection Question: What kind words can you share today, and how do they impact the people you speak to?

November 27th: Acts of Kindness in the Community

Community acts of kindness build stronger bonds. Today, focus on contributing to your community through kindness.

Participate in a community service activity, volunteer, or organize a small neighborhood event. Notice the sense of unity and positivity this brings.

Feel the joy of contributing to your community's well-being. Embrace the collective power of kindness.

Words of Wisdom: "The best way to find yourself is to lose yourself in the service of others." —Mahatma Gandhi

From the Bible: "Let us not become weary in doing good, for at the proper time we will reap a harvest if we do not give up." —Galatians 6:9

Reflection Question: How can you contribute to your community today, and what impact does it have on you and those around you?

November 28th: Spreading Love through Gratitude

Expressing gratitude is a powerful act of love. Today, focus on spreading love by expressing your gratitude to others.

Thank someone for their kindness, support, or presence in your life. Write a thank-you note, send a message, or tell them in person.

Notice how expressing gratitude strengthens your relationships and spreads warmth. Embrace gratitude as a way to share love.

Words of Wisdom: "Gratitude is a currency that we can mint for ourselves, and spend without fear of bankruptcy." —Fred De Witt Van Amburgh

From the Bible: ""Give thanks to Jehovah, for he is good; For his loyal love endures forever." —Psalm 136:1

Reflection Question: Who can you express gratitude to today, and how does this act of love enhance your connection with them?

November 29th: Forgiving with Love

Forgiveness is one of the purest forms of love. Today, focus on extending forgiveness to those who have wronged you, whether in small or significant ways.

Take time to reflect on any grudges or resentment you may be holding onto. Offer forgiveness in your heart, and if appropriate, reach out to express your forgiveness directly.

Notice the sense of peace and freedom that comes from letting go of bitterness and embracing forgiveness. Embrace the power of forgiveness as an act of love that heals both the giver and the receiver.

Words of Wisdom: "Forgiveness does not change the past, but it does enlarge the future." —Paul Boese

From the Bible: "Continue putting up with one another and forgiving one another freely even if anyone has a cause for complaint against another. Just as Jehovah freely forgave you, you must also do the same." —Colossians 3:13

Reflection Question: Who do you need to forgive today, and how can this act of love bring healing and peace to your life?

November 30th: Radiating Love Through Prayer

Prayer is a powerful way to radiate love into the world. Today, focus on offering prayers for those in need of love, healing, and support.

Spend time in prayer, asking Jehovah to bless others with love and strength. Whether you pray for your loved ones, your community, or those suffering worldwide, let your prayers be filled with compassion and love.

Notice the connection and peace that comes from praying for others. Embrace prayer as a means of spreading love beyond physical actions, knowing that your heartfelt prayers can make a difference.

Words of Wisdom: "When we pray, we open the door for God to enter our hearts and the lives of those we love." —Wayne Dyer, *There's a Spiritual Solution to Every Problem*

From the Bible: "Therefore, let us approach the throne of undeserved kindness with freeness of speech, so that we may receive mercy and find undeserved kindness to help us at the right time." —Hebrews 4:16

Reflection Question: Who can you pray for today, and how does offering these prayers deepen your sense of connection and love?

Conclusion

Congratulations on completing this year-long journey of personal inspiration and spiritual growth! Your dedication to engaging daily with these devotions is a testament to your commitment to self-discovery and improvement. Throughout this book, you have explored themes that touch the core of what it means to live a fulfilling and inspired life. From the quiet reflections of winter to the vibrant self-expression of summer, each season has offered unique insights and opportunities for growth. Let's take a moment to reflect on the key themes we've covered and the transformative power they hold.

This book has guided you through a year of seasons, each one symbolizing a different aspect of personal inspiration and spiritual growth. Let's reflect on these key themes and the invaluable lessons they brought.

Winter: Reflection and Inner Peace In the quiet of winter, we focused on reflection and finding inner peace. This season encouraged introspection, helping you to pause and look inward. Through daily practices like meditation and mindfulness, you cultivated a deeper understanding of yourself. The fruitage of the spirit here was Love, emphasizing the importance of self-love and acceptance as the foundation for all growth.

Spring: Renewal and Rebirth Spring brought the themes of renewal and rebirth. As nature awakens, so did your spirit. This season was about embracing new beginnings and setting intentions for personal growth. Joy was the guiding fruitage, encouraging you to find delight in fresh starts and the possibilities they bring. By nurturing seeds of intention, you prepared for the blossoming of new habits, relationships, and goals.

Summer: Radiance and Self-Expression Summer's warmth and light symbolized radiance and self-expression. This season encouraged you to step into your confidence and share your unique gifts with the world.

Peace was the fruitage of the spirit, highlighting the serenity that comes from being true to yourself and expressing your inner light. Through practices like creative pursuits and celebrating individuality, you learned to radiate your authentic self.

Autumn: Harvest and Gratitude Autumn focused on harvest and gratitude, a time to reflect on the abundance you've cultivated throughout the year. This season was about appreciating the fruits of your labor, both materially and spiritually. Kindness was the key fruitage, reminding you to extend gratitude and generosity to yourself and others. By acknowledging your growth and sharing your blessings, you embraced the interconnectedness of life and the ongoing cycle of giving and receiving.

Interconnected Themes These themes are interconnected, each one building upon the previous to create a continuous and evolving process of personal growth. Love laid the groundwork in winter, enabling the joy of spring's renewal. The confidence and peace of summer's self-expression were strengthened by the gratitude and kindness harvested in autumn. Together, these seasons have woven a holistic understanding of inspiration, demonstrating that personal growth is not a linear path but a dynamic and ever-evolving journey.

As you reflect on these themes, consider how they have interplayed in your life over the past year. Recognize that the lessons learned are not confined to a single season but are part of a lifelong practice of growth and self-improvement.

As you look back on this year, take a moment to reflect on your personal growth and transformation. Consider how your perceptions, attitudes, and behaviors have shifted through the seasons. What insights have you gained about yourself? Think about the challenges you faced and the triumphs you celebrated. Each obstacle was an opportunity to discover your inner strength and resilience.

Perhaps you found new ways to practice self-love, embraced new beginnings with joy, expressed your true self with confidence, or cultivated gratitude and kindness in your daily life. These moments of growth reveal the depth of your character and your capacity for change.

Reflect on the times you stumbled and how you picked yourself back up. Recognize the strength it took to keep moving forward. Your journey through this year has been a testament to your resilience and determination. As you continue on this path, remember that personal growth is an ongoing process. Each day brings new opportunities to learn, grow, and transform. Celebrate your progress and look forward to the endless possibilities ahead.

The journey of personal inspiration and spiritual growth doesn't end here. It's essential to continue the practices and insights you've gained throughout the year. Revisit the devotions that resonated most deeply with you, allowing their wisdom to deepen and expand within you. Keep the cycle of reflection and inspiration alive by setting new goals and intentions. Consider starting the book anew; you may find even deeper insights and growth the second time around. Each season, each devotion, offers layers of meaning and opportunities for further transformation. Your commitment to ongoing growth will keep your spirit vibrant and your life enriched with purpose and fulfillment. Continue to nurture your inner power and embrace each day as a new opportunity to live more fully and joyfully.

You possess incredible inner power and limitless potential. Remember, the journey of self-discovery and inspiration is never truly finished. Each day presents a new opportunity to live more fully, embrace joy, and explore the depths of your being. Trust in your strength and the wisdom you've cultivated. The possibilities ahead are endless, and you have the power to create a life filled with purpose and fulfillment.

About the Autor

Susan Wright brings years of ministry experience to the pages of *"The Power Within: 365-Day Devotional for Women."* Her journey has been one of profound spiritual discovery, focusing not just on what we say but more importantly on how we live for the greater good of others.

Susan has witnessed the struggles and burdens that women endure—often feeling overwhelmed by life's demands. Ordained three years ago, she felt a compelling need to share her wisdom with other women, to encourage and inspire, and most importantly, to plant seeds of love that will flourish both within them and in the wider world.

Susan lives on a farm in Montana, US, with her chickens and her dog, Jordy.

Please take a moment to ***write a review*** of this book and share your journey.

Also, look for her journal book:

" The Love Within: 365 Day Devotional Journal for Women "

Made in United States
Troutdale, OR
11/24/2024

25039469R00159